HOW TO PREPARE FOR THE
COMING
REVIVAL

HOW TO PREPARE FOR THE
COMING
REVIVAL

by

Richard Booker

Destiny Image Publishers
P.O. Box 351
Shippensburg, PA 17257
(717) 532-3040

Also by Richard Booker
Available from Destiny Image Publishers:

The Miracle of the Scarlet Thread
Come and Dine
Intimacy with God
Jesus in the Feasts of Israel
Seated in Heavenly Places
Blow the Trumpet in Zion
Radical Christian Living

Unless otherwise noted, Scripture references are from The New King James Bible, copyright © 1982, Thomas Nelson Inc., Nashville, Tn.

King James Version (KJV)

Revised Standard Version, copyright © 1973 (RSV)

How to Prepare for the Coming Revival
Copyright © 1990 by Sounds of the Trumpet, Inc.
Destiny Image Publishers
P.O. Box 351
Shippensburg, PA 17257

ISBN 1-56043-010-9

About the Author

Richard Booker is an author and Bible teacher presently living in Houston, Texas. His organization, Sounds of the Trumpet, Inc., provides Christian teachings through books, tapes, workshops, etc. Prior to his call to the teaching ministry, Richard was a computer and management consultant, climbing the corporate career ladder. His B.S. and M.B.A. degrees well prepared him. His career became his god, and he spent ten years chasing that elusive idol, dragging his wife, Peggy, across the country with him.

During that time he lectured throughout the United States, Canada and Mexico, training over one thousand management and computer personnel. His more than twenty articles appeared in the leading computer publications. He was listed in *Who's Who in Computers and Automation, Who's Who in Training and Development,* and *The Dictionary of International Biography,* and was a frequent speaker for the American Management Association.

In the middle 1970's God gave Richard an "Emmaus Road" experience that changed his life. He left his career to devote all his time to writing and teaching about God's Word. He has an international teaching ministry and is the author of numerous Christian books that have touched the lives of many thousands around the world. A list of Richard's Bible study materials is included in the back of this book.

CONTENTS

1

The Cry for Revival

In 1974, God dramatically changed my life and directed me to leave my successful business career to teach the Bible. Since that time, I have had the privilege of ministering God's Word in many Churches across America.

These Churches represent a broad cross section of Christian experience and expression. Some are denominational; others are independent. Some have a very formal order of worship in their services; others are spontaneous. There have been large Churches and small ones. Some have been affluent; others could barely pay their bills. I've ministered in Church facilities located in the cities, the suburbs and rural areas from one end of the land to the next.

In spite of their diversity, the people in these Churches have shown a common recognition of the great need and desire for revival in America. Throughout our great nation, there is a devout remnant of true believers who are crying out to God for revival.

I believe God is going to send revival to America. But what is revival and how do we prepare for it? That is the subject of this book.

What Is Revival?
Even though Christians agree that we need revival, very

few seem to know what revival is. They generally confuse it with evangelism.

Churches often schedule an evangelist to give a series of meetings for the purpose of preaching the gospel to the unsaved. They normally advertise these meetings as a "revival."

But evangelism is not revival! Genuine revival will produce evangelistic activities because a zeal to witness and a concern for souls is a natural overflow of revival.

Others think of revival as a series of meetings with an unusual display of supernatural signs and wonders such as healings, prophetic utterances and various manifestations of the gifts of the Holy Spirit. These demonstrations of God's power certainly accompany revival, but they themselves are not revival!

So what is revival? A definition of revival I like to use as it pertains to the Church is as follows: *Revival is a visitation from God that renews life in the Church and produces lasting moral change.*

I have included the three elements of revival in this definition. They are: 1) a visitation from God, 2) a renewing of life, and 3) a lasting moral change. Any religious happening that does not include these three elements is not true revival, even though it may be a positive experience and a great blessing to those who participate.

An Old Testament Scripture that helps us understand revival is Psalm 85:6. In this verse, we see the heart of one crying out to God for revival as many are today. His prayer to God was, "Will You not revive us again, that Your people may rejoice in You?"

This Scripture summarizes the basic concept of revival and how it works in our lives. In studying this verse, we learn six important features of revival.

1. Revival Comes from God

The first feature about revival is that it comes from God. The Psalmist realized that only God can bring about a revival. Man cannot create a revival through religious programs, spiritual conferences, large gatherings of believers, special anointed speakers, public relations or any other well-meaning effort.

2. We Can Prepare for Revival

The Psalmist recognized the need for revival and began to prepare for it through prayer (verse 6), obedience (verse 8), repentance (verse 8) and reverential fear (verse 9). Although God alone can send revival, we can prepare for revival so that God will send it in response to our desire and willingness to receive it.

3. God Has Sent Revival in the Past

Unfortunately, the Hebrews did not always walk with God as they should have. There were times when they forsook Him for the gods of their neighbors. Their religious apostasy was always followed by a decline in their morals, which had a devastating effect on the nation. They would then cry out for help to God, who, in His mercy, would send revival to the people.

The Church has not always been faithful to God either. There have been times when we have forsaken Him for our own gods. Our apostasy and indifference also have been followed by a decline in our morals, which we know has had a devastating effect on our nation.

Throughout the history of the Church, worldwide and in the United States, devout men and women have cried out to God during these times of moral despair. God had heard the cry of their hearts and sent revival to renew the Church and spare the nation. And God will do it again when we are willing to pay the price that is required.

4. Revival Is to the Church

A fourth feature of revival that is often misunderstood is that it comes to the people of God, not the people of the world. The Psalmist prayed for God to send revival to "Your people." He asked God to revive "us," not them.

Many Christians have the idea that revival is something God is going to send to the nation. They even pray, "O God, send revival to America." While we certainly want God to change the moral course of America, His primary concern is for the "Church in America." His intent is to revive the Church and then, by working through the Church, change the moral climate of the nation.

As we've learned through our definition, revival implies a renewing of life. You cannot renew to life something that has never lived. The Bible says that unbelievers are dead in their trespasses and sins (Eph. 2:1). The life of God is not in unbelievers, so it cannot be revived.

Where is God's life today on the earth? The Bible tells us that God lives in the hearts of all who have come to Him through Jesus Christ (1 Cor. 3:16; 6:19-20). He calls this company of people "the Church." We have a tendency to want God to revive "them," but we are the ones who need to be revived.

Paul used the Greek word that means revival when he wrote to Timothy, "Therefore I remind you to stir up the gift of God which is in you . . . " (2 Tim. 1:6)

The phrase "stir up" means to "fan into flame."

During the few cold nights we have in Houston, I enjoy making a fire in the fireplace in my living room. At first the fire is very hot and warms the entire room. But after awhile, the fire begins to die down. The logs do not burn as hot as they did at the beginning, and the room temperature cools. I must then get up from my comfortable chair and "stir the fire" until the logs once again burn hot. I have revived the fire.

In a similar way, the Church needs to be revived. When God first lights His fire in our hearts, it burns bright and hot, warming the souls of those around us with His love. But if we do not stay close to God, that fire within us will be diminished by the cares of the world, the lure of temptation and the trials of life. Our hearts will become cold and indifferent toward God. When this happens, we need God to stir the fire within us until we once again have a burning zeal for Him.

Jesus addressed this need with these words, "You are the light of the world. A city that is set on a hill cannot be hidden. Nor do they light a lamp and put it under a basket, but on a lampstand, and it gives light to all who are in the house. Let your light so shine before men, that they may see your good works and glorify your Father in heaven" (Matt. 5:14-16).

Many Christians are praying for revival in the White House. While we certainly want God to touch the lives of our political leaders, we must understand there will not be revival in the White House until we first have it in the Church House.

5. Revival Brings Rejoicing

Another feature of revival is that it always brings rejoicing to God's people. When there is a moral decline in the life of a nation or an individual, it will be accompanied by much sorrow and heartache. There will be mental confusion, which will lead to poor judgement and unsound decisions. There will be emotional instability and depression. The will becomes weak, resulting in the lack of courage and conviction. Health and prosperity will give way to sickness, disease and poverty.

But when God sends revival, His presence and His blessings are restored to the people, causing great rejoicing. King David understood this and prayed to God, "Restore to me the joy of Your salvation" (Ps. 51:12).

David also said to God, "You will show me the path of life; in Your presence is fullness of joy; at Your right hand are pleasures forevermore" (Ps. 16:11).

Isaiah wrote that God would give us " . . . beauty for ashes, the oil of joy for mourning, the garment of praise for the spirit of heaviness . . . " (Isa. 61:3)

Peter expressed this so well with the following words, "Repent therefore and be converted, that your sins may be blotted out, so that times of refreshing may come from the presence of the Lord" (Acts 3:19).

6. Revival Reveals God

The primary purpose of revival is to manifest the glory of God so that people will turn to Him and worship Him.

The Bible tells us there is a God in heaven who wants us to know Him, worship Him and serve Him. He has revealed Himself to us primarily in four ways. These are: 1) creation, 2) instinct, 3) the Bible, and 4) Jesus Christ. Whenever mankind turns his back on this revelation of God's existence and character, God makes Himself known in a fifth way — through revival.

In a revival, God moves in sovereign power by His Spirit to reveal His greatness and goodness to mankind. He does not make Himself known in order to promote a religious denomination, to substantiate religious doctrines or creeds, to further religious programs or to exalt human personalities. He alone is glorified, and every philosophy, person and program is overwhelmed by Him and His awesome holiness.

The prophet Habakkuk expressed the impact true revival

has on God's people and the world with these words, "But the LORD is in His holy temple. Let all the earth keep silence before Him" (Hab. 2:20).

Dear reader, do you need a time of refreshing from the Lord? Do want to see His glory? Does your heart cry out to God, "Will You not revive us again, so that Your people may rejoice in You"? Recognizing this important need in our lives today, let's now learn together how we can prepare ourselves for a visitation from God and the coming revival!

Chapter 1 — The Cry for Revival
Study Guide 1

1. Write your own definition of revival.

2. What are the three essential elements of revival?

3. List the six features of revival.

4. How can you apply this knowledge to your life?

2

Understanding the Fear of the Lord

One of the most important subjects in the Bible is the "fear of the Lord." It is perhaps the primary means through which God brings revival into the hearts of His people. Yet, for a long time, we Christians in the West have misunderstood and ignored this aspect of walking with God.

As a human father requires his children to honor and respect him, so God requires no less from His children. It is normal for a father to teach his children to fear him. So it is with God. In Psalm 34:11, God says to us, "Come, you children, listen to me; I will teach you the fear of the LORD."

Sometimes a father finds it necessary to remind his children to fear him. If a child is going to have a wholesome relationship with Dad, he or she will receive that instruction gladly. The same is true for the children of God. Psalm 86:11 expresses what our attitude should be concerning this instruction from our heavenly Father. It says, "Teach me Your way, O LORD; I will walk in Your truth; unite my heart to fear Your name."

I believe we are living in the time and season when God wants to remind us to fear Him. My prayer is that this book will lovingly encourage you to respond to Him in a positive way, so that our hearts will be united to honor, respect and obey God as we should.

God's One Requirement

Because God made us, He certainly knows how easy it is for us to get distracted. He knows that we can often lose our perspective of what is really important. In view of these human tendencies, we are constantly reminded in the Bible to fear the Lord. God's reminders are too numerous to list, but here are a few.

And now, Israel, what does the LORD your God require of you, but to fear the LORD your God, to walk in all His ways and to love Him, to serve the LORD your God with all your heart and with all your soul (Deut. 10:12).

You shall walk after the LORD your God and fear Him, and keep His commandments and obey His voice, and you shall serve Him and hold fast to Him (Deut. 13:4).

Now therefore, fear the LORD, serve Him in sincerity and truth . . . (Josh. 24:14)

Let all the earth fear the LORD; Let all the inhabitants of the world stand in awe of Him (Ps. 33:8).

Do not let your heart envy sinners, but be zealous for the fear of the LORD all the day (Prov. 23:17).

Therefore, having these promises, beloved, let us cleanse ourselves from all filthiness of the flesh and spirit, perfecting holiness in the fear of God (2 Cor. 7:1).

. . . work out your own salvation with fear and trembling (Phil. 2:12).

Therefore, since we are receiving a kingdom which cannot be shaken, let us have grace, by which we may serve God acceptably with reverence and godly fear (Heb. 12:28).

. . . Fear God and give glory to Him, for the hour of His judgement has come . . . (Rev. 14:7)

From these and many other Scriptures, we learn that God, like any human father, delights in His children when they serve Him with reverence and fear. But what does it mean to fear the Lord?

The Meaning of Fear

The word "fear" as it is used in the Bible has both a negative and a positive use. The negative use of the word basically means to be afraid, alarmed, intimidated, threatened, frightened, terrified and scared out of your wits so that you run from danger.

This negative kind of fear was first experienced by man when Adam and Eve sinned. They hid from God because their sin made them fear God in an unhealthy, unwholesome, negative way. So when God came in His love to restore Adam to fellowship, Adam told God that he had run and hidden because he was afraid of God. (See Genesis 3:10.)

Before Adam and Eve sinned, they feared God in the positive sense of the word. But afterwards, their wholesome reverence for God turned to terror. Fear is the natural consequence of sin. Since Adam is the father of the human race, we have all inherited from him the same negative understanding and feeling concerning the fear of God. We think that God is a danger we should run from. So we hide from Him in the little gardens we create for ourselves. Then when God comes to restore us, we run deeper into the thickness of the trees and bushes of this world, hoping God won't find us.

Not only did sin introduce a negative fear of God, it also produced in us an unwholesome fear of people, things and circumstances.

11

People are afraid of one another. They are afraid of what someone might think or say about them, or do to them. Jacob asked God to save him from his brother Esau, whom he had earlier cheated, because he was afraid of Esau. And rightly so! (See Genesis 32:11.)

Sin has produced a negative fear in the hearts of all mankind. This wrong kind of fear is often the primary emotion, force and motivation governing our relationships with God and each other.

Not only do we have this negative fear relationship with God and people, we also have it with things, circumstances and the unknown. We even have a special word to identify these fears. We call them "phobias."

I live in Houston, Texas. There are people here who are terrified of driving on the freeways; they have what's been diagnosed as "freeway phobia." If you've ever driven the freeways of Houston, or any other large city, you can understand why.

The Bible says the world will become so bound by fear that people will die of heart attacks brought on by the fear itself. (See Luke 21:26.)

Human history, and our own personal experiences, teach us that this negative type of fear is destructive. When the Bible speaks to us about this fear, we are told to put it out of our lives.

God said it this way through the prophet Isaiah, "Fear not, for I am with you; be not dismayed, for I am your God. I will strengthen you, yes, I will help you; I will uphold you with My righteous right hand" (Isa. 41:10).

Paul wrote these words to Timothy, "For God has not given us a spirit of fear, but of power and of love and of a sound mind" (2 Tim. 1:7).

John gave this word of comfort about God's love, "There is no fear in love; but perfect love casts out fear, because fear involves torment. But he who fears has not been made perfect in love" (1 John 4:18).

God does not want us tormented by this negative type of fear towards Him, other people, or circumstances in life. So when the Bible speaks about fearing God, it does not mean this kind of fear. What then does it mean?

Positive Fear

There is a positive use of the word "fear" in the Bible that is rarely used today. Basically, it means to show proper respect and honor to a position or person that is greater than you or has authority over you. We read, for example, in the Bible, "On that day the LORD exalted Joshua in the sight of all Israel; and they feared him, as they feared Moses, all the days of his life" (Josh. 4:14).

If you had an audience with the president of the United States, you would certainly show honor and respect to him. You would do this because of the position he holds, even if you didn't like the person as an individual.

The presidency of the United States represents the full power, might and authority of the nation, and that is a power to be feared, that is, honored and respected. At the time of this writing, George Bush is the president of the United States. If you went to the White House, you would not call him George. You would call him "Mr. President."

Since we give this much respect and honor to human power and authority, how much more should we give it to God, who is the supreme authority and power in the universe.

With this thought in mind, consider the following meaning of the word "fear" as it applies to God:

13

The fear of the Lord is a deep abiding reverence for God that is the primary motivation and controlling factor in our lives causing us to want to please Him in word, thought and deed.

We see that this is not the negative type of fear we've already discussed, but a healthy, wholesome reverence for God. This fear of the Lord should be the ruling force in our lives. It not only governs our relationship with God, but our relationships with one another as well.

This positive fear of the Lord is manifested in our lives through the way we live. If we fear Him in this wholesome sense, we will keep His commandments, walk in His ways, do His will, turn from our sins, and lead a life that honors God.

The Psalmist said it well with these words, "For who in the heavens can be compared to the LORD? Who among the sons of the mighty can be likened to the LORD? God is greatly to be feared in the assembly of the saints, and to be held in reverence by all those around Him" (Ps. 89:6-7).

When Is Fear Not Fear?

There are a number of instances in the Bible where both the negative and positive uses of the word "fear" are found. Abraham is one example. God said to him, " . . . 'Do not be **afraid** [fear not], Abram. I am your shield, your **exceedingly** great reward' " (Gen. 15:1). Here we see the negative use of the word.

Yet, on another occasion, God spoke these words to Abraham, " . . . 'Do not lay your hand on the lad, or do anything to him; for now I know that you fear God . . . ' " (Gen. 22:12). This was a word of positive encouragement from God to Abraham because of his obedience.

When Paul was in jail in Rome, his presence and witness

greatly encouraged the other believers to speak God's word without fear (Phil. 1:14). This is the negative use of the word. Yet, a few verses later, he told them to work out their salvation with fear and trembling (Phil. 2:12) — the positive use.

Results of Not Fearing God

Unfortunately, there is little or no positive fear of God in our nation today. It saddens me to say this is also true in the Church.

What are the results of not fearing God? We kill millions of pre-born babies, all in the name of individual rights. We pass laws to protect sexual perverts. We condone immorality and homosexuality. We give "live-in partners" the same rights as a husband and wife, and recognize them as a family unit. We are plagued with new diseases caused by our sins. Our children's lives are destroyed by drugs, while many who graduate from school can barely read and write.

The nation is bankrupt, with a national debt that is sapping the economic strength of the country. Many of our leaders in government are interested only in themselves, rather than serving the people who elected them.

Our financial institutions are failing at an alarming rate. Our military weapons are unreliable, because they are made with inferior parts.

The Church has been more influenced by the world than the world by the Church. According to a recent Gallup poll, only twelve percent of the professing Christians in America say their beliefs influence their daily lives. Only a godly remnant of true believers give their time, talents and money to the work of God. The rest live a life of self-indulgence, and you can hardly distinguish them from the nonbelievers.

We learn from the following Scriptures that sin abounds where there is no fear of God.

Transgression speaks to the wicked deep in his heart; there is no fear of God before his eyes (Ps. 36:1, RSV). (See also Romans 3:10-18.)

Blessed is the man who fears the LORD always; but he who hardens his heart will fall into calamity (Prov. 28:14, RSV).

Your own wickedness will correct you, and your back-slidings will rebuke you. Know therefore and see that it is an evil and bitter thing that you have forsaken the LORD your God, and the fear of Me is not in you . . . (Jer. 2:19)

Because they hated knowledge and did not choose the fear of the LORD, they would have none of My counsel and despised My every rebuke (Prov. 1:29-30).

The Fear of God — Our Only Hope

An understanding and personal experience of the fear of God is our only hope for revival in our hearts, our families, our Churches, our cities and our nation. This is confirmed by the following Scriptures.

Do not fear [negative]*; for God has come to test you, and that His fear* [positive] *may be before you, so that you may not sin* (Ex. 20:20).

Oh, that they had such a heart in them that they would fear Me and always keep all My commandments, that it might be well with them and with their children forever! (Deut. 5:29)

Better is a little with the fear of the LORD, than great treasure with trouble (Prov. 15:16).

. . . And by the fear of the LORD one departs from evil (Prov. 16:6).

. . . I will put My fear in their hearts so that they will not depart from Me (Jer. 32:40).

Learning to Fear God

How do we learn to fear God? By knowing Him! We know a lot about God and the things He does. But our knowledge of God Himself is very superficial. To know God is to fear Him. We must learn who God is in His personality, His greatness and His character.

How do we get to know God in this way? We come to know God intimately by studying what He tells us about Himself in the Bible.

God gave the king of Israel (the government) the following instructions: "Also it shall be, when he sits on the throne of his kingdom, that he shall write for himself a copy of this law in a book, from the one before the priests, the Levites. And it shall be with him, and he shall read it all the days of his life, that he may learn to fear the LORD his God and be careful to observe all the words of this law and these statutes" (Deut. 17:18-19).

Then God told the king to read His Word to all the people: "When all Israel comes to appear before the LORD your God in the place which He chooses, you shall read this law before all Israel in their hearing. Gather the people together, men and women and little ones, and the stranger who is within your gates, that they may hear and that they may learn to fear the LORD your God and carefully observe all the words of this law, and that their children, who have not known it, may hear and learn to fear the LORD your God as long as you live in the land which you cross the Jordan to possess" (Deut. 31:11-13).

King Solomon adds the following concerning God's Word, "If you seek her as silver, and search for her as for hidden treasures; then you will understand the fear of the LORD, and find the knowledge of God" (Prov. 2:4-5).

God's way of reviving and keeping a high spiritual and moral level in nations and individual lives is by developing an understanding and practice of godly fear. This happens when we find the knowledge of God Himself through reading the Bible.

As we focus our thoughts on God, His blazing glory and dazzling beauty overwhelms us. His spectacular splendor and wonderful wisdom burn in our hearts. His greatness and goodness and majesty and mercy draw us to Himself. His power and purity cleanse us from sin and make us whole.

If you have a need for a deeper knowledge of God, I encourage you to read my book, *Intimacy with God*, which is available through this ministry. It will give you a clear understanding of who God really is, and how you can know Him more personally to develop a wholesome fear of Him.

Benefits of Fearing God

There are many Christians who have discovered that God is a loving God who wants to bless them. Sometimes in their enthusiasm, they give more attention to the blessings than they do to God. But God, Himself, is the source of all blessings.

The Bible promises more benefits for the person who fears Him than it does for any other aspect of our walk with God. There are too many promises to list all of them, but I have grouped the following into fifteen categories so you can easily understand them.

1. Great Blessings

Blessed is every one who fears the LORD, who walks in His ways. Behold, thus shall the man be blessed who fears the LORD (Ps. 128:1,4).

He will bless those who fear the LORD, both small and great (Ps. 115:13).

18

Blessed is the man who fears the LORD . . . (Ps. 112:1)

Oh, that they had such a heart in them that they would fear Me and always keep all My commandments, that it might be well with them and their children forever (Deut. 5:29).

2. A Long, Rewarding, Satisfied Life

The fear of the LORD prolongs days, But the years of the wicked will be shortened (Prov. 10:27).

The fear of the LORD is a fountain of life, to turn one away from the snares of death (Prov. 14:27).

The fear of the LORD leads to life, And he who has it will abide in satisfaction; he will not be visited with evil (Prov. 19:23).

By humility and the fear of the LORD are riches and honor and life (Prov. 22:4).

3. God's Provisions

Behold, the eye of the LORD is on those who fear Him, on those who hope in His mercy, to deliver their soul from death, and to keep them alive in famine (Ps. 33:18-19).

Oh, fear the LORD, you His saints! There is no want to those who fear Him (Ps. 34:9).

He has given food to those who fear Him . . . (Ps. 111:5)

4. Deliverance and Protection

But the LORD your God you shall fear; and He will

19

deliver you from the hand of all your enemies (2 Kings 17:39).

The angel of the LORD encamps all around those who fear Him, and delivers them (Ps. 34:7).

You who fear the LORD, trust in the LORD; He is their help and their shield (Ps. 115:11).

In the fear of the LORD there is strong confidence, and His children will have a place of refuge (Prov. 14:26).

5. Health and Healing

Do not be wise in your own eyes; fear the LORD and depart from evil. It will be health to your flesh, and strength to your bones (Prov. 3:7-8).

6. Divine Guidance

Who is the man that fears the LORD? Him shall He teach in the way He chooses (Ps. 25:12).

7. Prosperity

He himself shall dwell in prosperity, and his descendants shall inherit the earth (Ps. 25:13).

By humility and the fear of the LORD are riches and honor and life (Prov. 22:4).

8. Desires of Your Heart

He will fulfill the desire of those who fear Him; He also will hear their cry and save them (Ps. 145:19).

9. Special Promise to Women

A. Fruitfulness

But the midwives feared God, and did not do as the king of Egypt commanded them, but let the male children live. And because the midwives feared God he gave them families (Ex. 1:17,21, RSV).

B. Praise
Charm is deceitful and beauty is passing, but a woman who fears the LORD, she shall be praised (Prov. 31:30).

10. *True Wisdom and Knowledge*

The fear of the LORD is the beginning of knowledge . . . (Prov. 1:7)

The fear of the Lord is the beginning of wisdom, and the knowledge of the Holy One is understanding (Prov. 9:10).

The fear of the LORD is the instruction of wisdom (Prov. 15:33).

The fear of the LORD is the beginning of wisdom; a good understanding have all those who do His commandments (Ps. 111:10).

11. *Forgiveness*

If You, LORD, should mark iniquities, O LORD, who could stand? But there is forgiveness with You, that You may be feared (Ps. 130:3-4).

12. *Communion with God*

The secret of the LORD is with those who fear Him, and He will show them His covenant (Ps. 25:14).

13. *Supernatural Visitations*
There was a certain man in Caesarea called Cornelius

. . . a devout man and one who feared God with all his household, who gave alms generously to the poor, and prayed to God always (Acts 10:1-2). (See also Acts 10:3-48.)

14. Remembrance before God

Then those who feared the LORD spoke to one another, and the LORD listened and heard them; so a book of remembrance was written before Him for those who fear the LORD and who meditate on His name (Mal. 3:16).

15. Revival

Surely His salvation is near to those who fear Him, that glory may dwell in our land (Ps. 85:9).

The fear of the LORD is to hate evil (Prov. 8:13).

. . . and by the fear of the LORD one departs from evil (Prov. 16:6).

In Conclusion

King Solomon was perhaps the richest and wisest man who ever lived. He had opportunity to experience all that life had to offer. Yet he found life empty of meaning, purpose and true satisfaction when lived without God. He finally came to the following conclusion, " . . . Fear God, and keep His commandments; for this is the whole duty of man" (Eccl. 12:13, RSV).

Chapter 2 — Understanding the Fear of the Lord
Study Guide 2

1. What does it mean to "fear the Lord"?

2. What happens when we don't fear the Lord?

3. How do we learn to fear the Lord?

4. List the benefits of fearing God.

5. Determine what you must do to develop a positive fear of God in your own life. How can you share this with others?

3

Rejoicing in Repentance

A person who sincerely fears God will gladly turn from his or her sins. That's why I have entitled this chapter "Rejoicing in Repentance." That's a curious title because people don't normally think of repentance as something to rejoice about. The word "repentance" has a very negative meaning for us. We think of it as a thing to dread and avoid at all cost. Yet Jesus said we should rejoice when one sinner repents (Luke 15:7,10).

How can repentance be good news? Because it is through repentance that God is able to bless us with His divine presence. It is through repentance that God is able to give us a time of refreshing and stir the flame within us with revival fire.

When God formed Adam from the dust of the earth, He created him as a triune being with a spirit, a soul and a body (Gen. 2:7; 1 Thess. 5:23). Before Adam sinned, he had perfect fellowship with God and enjoyed the abundance of God's blessings. But when he sinned, Adam lost this fellowship with God. His spirit became dead to God, his soul became vulnerable to Satanic oppression and his body began to die.

Since Adam is the father of the human race, we have inherited this unfortunate condition from him. (See Romans 5:17-21.) We too have a spirit that is dead to God and enslaved by terrible attitudes and habits that destroy us. We too suffer in our soul with mental anguish, emotional depression and a weak will that yields to temptation. And we all live in human bodies that are so easily susceptible to sickness, disease and death.

The Bible tells us that through the gift of repentance offered to us by God we can change these tragic circumstances in our lives. In regard to our spirit, we can have our sins forgiven and once again enjoy the presence of God.

The apostle Peter, who experienced this forgiveness in his own life, wrote these words, which I previously mentioned, "Repent therefore and be converted, that your sins may be blotted out, so that times of refreshing may come from the presence of the Lord" (Acts 3:19).

The gift of repentance also enables us to be liberated from Satanic oppression and spiritual strongholds that torment our minds, cripple our emotions and take captive our wills. We can benefit in our bodies with health and healing.

Mark 6:12-13 says it this way, "So they went out and preached that people should repent. And they cast out many demons, and anointed with oil many who were sick, and healed them."

The gift of repentance can bring life to our spirits, freedom to our souls, and health to our bodies. With this positive view of repentance, we can see that it is certainly good news. But what is repentance and how does it work in our lives?

The True Meaning of Repentance

We may define repentance as the grace of God applied to our lives, causing us to change the way we think and act.

Repentance involves turning from a life that leads us away from God, to a life that leads us towards God. It is a turning from any word, thought or deed that would lead us away from God, to words, thoughts and deeds that lead us towards God.

Repentance is not lamenting, remorse or regret. Consider this classic family situation when Mom has told the children not to eat any more cookies. Yet, the temptation is just too much for them to resist. As soon as Mom leaves the room and the way is clear, the kids head straight for the cookie jar. And you know what happens next. Mom returns and "catches them in the act."

The children freeze! But then they gain their senses and tell Mom how sorry they are and that they'll never do it again (which Mom quickly recognizes as a ploy to avoid a spanking). The reason she so quickly recognizes it is because she told her Mom the same story.

Now every insightful parent, even the most novice, knows that the children are not sorry because they put their hands in the cookie jar. They're sorry because they got caught!

I've ministered to many people over the years who were sorry about the consequences of sin in their lives. They were even sorry (regretful) about the sin. But they would not turn away from their sins. True repentance, as offered in the Bible, requires a change both in attitude and action.

John the Baptist said it in these words, "Therefore bear fruits worthy of repentance" (Matt. 3:8). (See also Luke 3:8.)

When Paul defended himself against King Agrippa, he summarized his message to both the Jews and Gentiles by saying " . . . that they should repent, turn to God, and do works befitting repentance" (Acts 26:20).

The Necessity of Repentance

The Bible speaks about repentance a lot more than we do. In fact, the word "repent" in its various forms is mentioned in the Bible 110 times.

In the Old Testament, the prophet Amos said there would be a famine in the land. He explained this would not be a famine of food but a famine of God's Word. He went on to say that many would travel long distances seeking the Word of the Lord, but they would not find it. (See Amos 8:11-12.) This covered a period of approximately 400 years.

If the president of the United States didn't address the nation during his entire term of office, people would do everything they could to get him to speak. Then if he finally broke his silence, the whole world would listen to see what he would say.

After 400 years, God finally broke His silence. He held a press conference and sent a fellow named John the Baptist as His spokesman. Here is what God had to say through John, "Repent, for the kingdom of heaven is at hand!" (Matt. 3:2)

Isn't that interesting? After 400 years of silence, the only thing God had to say was "repent." That's certainly not what the people wanted to hear. It seems like God could have said something more uplifting than "repent."

There are a lot of Christians in our world today who have not heard from God in a long time. They go from meeting to meeting and conference to conference, following their favorite teacher, hoping to get a Word from God. It just may be that the simple word God has for them is — repent!

Jesus began His ministry with the same message. Matthew wrote, "From that time Jesus began to preach and to say, 'Repent, for the kingdom of heaven is at hand' " (Matt. 4:17).

At another time Jesus said, "I have not come to call the righteous, but sinners, to repentance" (Luke 5:32).

Luke also records these words of Jesus, "...Unless you repent you will all likewise perish" (Luke 13:3,5).

Later, when Jesus sent out His twelve disciples to minister, they also preached that people should repent. (See Mark 6:12.)

On the Day of Pentecost, Peter gave a powerful sermon that greatly convicted the people of their sins. When they asked him what they should do, he said, "Repent, and let every one of you be baptized in the name of Jesus Christ for the remission of sins; and you shall receive the gift of the Holy Spirit" (Acts 2:38).

Years later, with the need for repentance still burning in his heart, Peter wrote, "The Lord is not slack concerning His promise, as some count slackness, but is longsuffering toward us, not willing that any should perish but that all should come to repentance" (2 Pet. 3:9).

Paul preached the same message and reminded the elders of the church in Ephesus "how I kept back nothing that was helpful, but proclaimed it to you, and taught you publicly and from house to house, testifying to Jews, and also to Greeks, repentance toward God and faith toward our Lord Jesus Christ" (Acts 20:20-21).

He said to the men of Athens, "...Now God commands all men everywhere to repent" (Acts 17:30).

Jesus instructed the Churches in the book of Revelation to repent of their shortcomings. (See Revelation 2-3.)

The Working of Repentance

As I have mentioned, God created us as triune beings with a spirit, soul and body. Repentance works in our soul, which is our mind, emotions and will. It is produced in us by the Holy Spirit (John 16:8).

The Mind

The Holy Spirit begins His work of repentance in our minds. He renews our minds in order to bring about a change in our thinking.

Jesus gave us a parable to illustrate this. He told a story about a father who instructed his two sons to go work in the field. The first son said he would not go, but later changed his mind and went. The second son said that he would go, but did not. (See Matthew 21:28-31.)

Jesus said the first son changed his mind and went. This is true repentance. Repentance produces a change in our thinking that leads to a change in our actions. And as I said, it begins in our minds.

As we meditate on God and His Word, the Holy Spirit reveals to us what God considers to be right and wrong in our lives. We learn this from the following Scriptures.

Open my eyes, that I may see wondrous things from Your law (Ps. 119:18).

How can a young man cleanse his way? By taking heed according to Your word (Ps. 119:9).

Your word I have hidden in my heart, that I might not sin against You (Ps. 119:11).

The Holy Spirit renews our minds through God's Word, producing in us the mind of Christ. The result is that we no longer think worldly self-centered thoughts, but our minds are filled with the thoughts of God.

The Emotions

As the Holy Spirit produces these thoughts in our minds, He then convicts our emotions so that we desire to turn from the negative, destructive forces in our lives to the positive graces of God. The following Scriptures confirm this process.

With my whole heart I have sought You; Oh, let me not wander from Your commandments! (Ps. 119:10)

I will delight myself in Your statutes; I will not forget Your word (Ps. 119:16).

For godly sorrow produces repentance leading to salvation, not to be regretted; but the sorrow of the world produces death (2 Cor. 7:10).

The Will

Once the Holy Spirit convicts our emotions, He then empowers our wills so that we can change our attitudes and actions. As we are learning, unless we have changed, we have not truly repented. We see this clearly stated in the following Scriptures.

Therefore I direct my steps by all thy precepts; I hate every false way (Ps. 119:128, RSV).

Direct my steps by Your word, and let no iniquity have dominion over me (Ps. 119:133).

Therefore, my beloved, as you have always obeyed, not as in my presence only, but now much more in my absence, work out your own salvation with fear and trembling; for it is God who works in you both to will and to do for His good pleasure (Phil. 2:12-13).

A Wayward Son

The classic illustration of this process in the Bible is the story of the "Prodigal Son" which Jesus tells and is recorded in Luke 15:11-32.

In this story, a man had two sons. The younger son demanded his inheritance, and after receiving it, traveled far away where he foolishly wasted all his money on worldly pleasures. About the same time he had spent all his money, a famine swept through the land. The young man found himself with no money, no friends and no job.

He was finally able to get work feeding the hogs at a local farm. He was so destitute and hungry that even the slop he fed the hogs looked good to him. But no one would help him.

It was at this low point in his life that the wayward son began to repent. We read in Luke 15:17, "But when he came to himself he said, 'How many of my father's hired servants have bread enough and to spare, but I perish here with hunger!' " (RSV)

Jesus said the young man "came to himself." This means he began to think about his situation. His mind was being renewed. We would say that he came to his senses. Perhaps he thought that Dad wasn't so bad after all. A change was taking place in his thinking.

The more he thought about Dad and his own condition, the more he realized how foolish he had been. He was then convicted in his emotions. He said to himself, "I will arise and go to my father, and I will say to him, 'Father, I have sinned against heaven and before you; I am no longer worthy to be called your son; treat me as one of your hired servants' " (Luke 15:18-19, RSV).

Jesus was careful to point out that the young man acknowledged his sin against God and his father. He was sorry for his sin and the unfortunate consequences of his life. Yet, if he had been only sorry and had not done anything about it, he just would have been lamenting, not repenting.

But this story has a happy ending. The next verse tells us, "And he arose and came to his father. But while he was yet at a distance, his father saw him and had compassion, and ran and embraced him and kissed him" (Luke 15:20, RSV).

The young man not only changed his mind, he also changed his actions. He left the rebellious life he had been living and returned to his father, who had been waiting to receive him with a father's love.

And, you know, our heavenly Father is waiting for us to come to our senses regarding those things in our lives that do not please Him. He desires to grant us the gift of repentance as we change our thinking and inner feelings, and return to Him with our whole heart. He receives us with perfect love, and that is the good news of repentance.

What Should We Repent From?

Sometimes we find ourselves in the same situation as the "Prodigal Son." We too must repent in order to receive the fullest of God's blessings. There are many things we should repent from, but the Bible clearly mentions the following seven areas of repentance.

1. Wicked Ways

. . . if My people who are called by My name will humble themselves, and pray and seek My face, and turn from their wicked ways, then I will hear from heaven, and will forgive their sin and heal their land (2 Chron. 7:14).

2. Worldliness

Do not love the world or the things in the world. If anyone loves the world, the love of the Father is not in him. For all that is in the world—the lust of the flesh, the lust of the eyes, and the pride of life—is not of the Father but is of the world. And the world is passing away, and the lust of it; but he who does the will of God abides forever (1 John 2:15-17).

3. Satanic Powers

. . . to open their eyes, in order to turn them from dark-ness to light, and from the power of Satan to God, that they

may receive forgiveness of sins and an inheritance among those who are sanctified by faith in Me (Acts 26:18).

4. Idolatry

Little children, keep yourselves from idols . . . (1 John 5:21)

5. Lukewarmness

I know your works, that you are neither cold nor hot. I wish you were cold or hot. So then, because you are lukewarm, and neither cold nor hot, I will vomit you out of my mouth. As many as I love, I rebuke and chasten. Therefore be zealous and repent (Rev. 3:15-16,19)

6. Lack of Love

Nevertheless I have this against you, that you have left your first love. Remember therefore from where you have fallen; repent and do the first works, or else I will come to you quickly and remove your lampstand from its place—unless you repent (Rev. 2:4-5).

7. Anti-Semitism

For behold, in those days and at that time, when I bring back the captives of Judah and Jerusalem, I will also gather all nations, and bring them down to the valley of Jehoshaphat; and I will enter into judgement with them there on account of My people, My heritage Israel, whom they have scattered among the nations . . . (Joel 3:1-2)

As a concluding thought on this brief study on repentance, let us heed the following words from the prophet Isaiah, "Seek the LORD while He may be found, call upon Him while He is near. Let the wicked forsake his way, and the unrighteous man his thoughts; let him return to the LORD, and He will have mercy on him; and to our God, for He will abundantly pardon" (Isa. 5:6-7).

Chapter 3 — Rejoicing in Repentance
Study Guide 3

1. Write your own definition of repentance.

2. Explain why it is necessary to repent.

3. Describe how repentance works in our lives.

4. List the seven areas of repentance mentioned in the Bible.

5. Ask God to show you areas of your life where repentance is needed.

4

Walking the Highway of Holiness

Isaiah predicted that a future prophet would come with a special message to prepare people for the coming of the Lord. Isaiah said this special messenger would preach the following sermon, " . . . Prepare the way of the LORD; make straight in the desert a highway for our God. Every valley shall be exalted, and every mountain and hill brought low; the crooked places shall be made straight, and the rough places smooth; the glory of the LORD shall be revealed, and all flesh shall see it together; for the mouth of the LORD has spoken" (Isa. 40:3-5).

Isaiah gave us a wonderful promise that God desires to reveal His glory to us. He wants the opportunity to give us a revelation of His blazing glory and dazzling beauty. He desires to overwhelm us with His greatness and goodness. He yearns to show us His majesty and mercy. He desires that we experience His power and purity. He delights in revealing His spectacular splendor and wonderful wisdom. He wants to share His charisma and character with all who will seek Him with their whole heart.

Isaiah used a natural explanation to teach us how God can do this. He mentioned a highway to be built just for God.

Usually, when a visiting dignitary goes to a certain city, a special route is prepared for him on which he will travel. Normally, the television news media will show the motorcade going down that special route to its final destination. The crowds of people line the streets hoping to get a glimpse of the person. But they can't get too close because the local authorities place barricades along the route to keep the people at a distance. Only the few people who know the person can come into his presence.

In a similar way, Isaiah mentions a highway or route prepared just for God to travel on as He seeks to come to us. Isaiah even gives us the name of this highway so we can know the route God will take. He says, "A highway shall be there, and a road, and it shall be called the Highway of Holiness. The unclean shall not pass over it, but it shall be for others . . . " (Isa. 35:8)

We learn from Isaiah that this highway is called the "highway of holiness." This is the road God travels on to come to us. It is also the road we must travel on to come to Him. Although there are many people who desire to get close to God, the various barricades of worldliness and moral uncleanness keep them away. Only when we walk in holiness can we come into God's presence and see His glory.

The Meaning of Holiness

The greatest desire of my heart is to be in the presence of God and behold His glory. If you want this as well, then make the journey with me on the highway of holiness.

The book of Leviticus probably deals more with God's holiness than any other book in the Bible. God gave these words to Moses, "Speak to all the congregation of the children of Israel, and say to them: 'You shall be holy, for I the LORD your God am holy' " (Leviticus 19:2). (See also Leviticus 11:44-45 and 20:7.)

The apostle Peter referred to these Scriptures in his New Testament writing and said, "but as He who called you is holy, you also be holy in all your conduct, because it is written, 'Be holy, for I am holy'." (1 Pet. 1:15-16).

A continuous theme running throughout the Bible is the revelation that God is holy. In order for us to know Him and walk with Him, we too must be holy. But what does it mean to be holy?

The most basic definition I can give you for the word "holy" is that it means "separate." For the believer, it is a separating from the world to God. This is both a state of being or standing the believer has with God, as well as an ongoing process being worked out in the believer's life. As a Christian, it is not only who you are that is important, but also who you are becoming. You are holy, and you're becoming holy.

God Is Holy

Why does God say we are to be holy? Because He Himself is holy. You see, what it means to belong to God depends on the nature of the God to whom you belong. Belonging to God means likeness to Him or imitating Him. Because God is holy, we are to be holy.

The creator God is separate or different from His creation. When we apply the word "holy" to God, it means that He is different from us in both His greatness and His moral character.

God spoke of His holy nature through Isaiah with these words, " 'For My thoughts are not your thoughts, nor are your ways My ways,' says the LORD. 'For as the heavens are higher than the earth, so are My ways higher than your ways, and My thoughts than your thoughts' " (Isa. 55:8-9).

When God delivered the Hebrews from Egypt, they sang, "Who is like You, O LORD, among the gods? Who is like You, glorious in holiness . . . " (Ex. 15:11)

39

Now you would think they would sing, "God, You are glorious in power," because it was God's power that delivered them from Egypt. But it was His holiness that distinguished Him. He was not like any of the other gods they knew. He was different. Later, a Hebrew woman named Hanna sang, "No one is holy like the LORD . . . " (1 Sam. 2:2)

It seems the main problem with the Hebrews (and us) was that they kept forgetting that God is holy. God chastised them one time with these words, "These things you have done and I have been silent; you thought that I was one like yourself. But now I rebuke you, and lay the charge before you" (Ps. 50:21, RSV).

To help them remember, the Hebrews even made up songs about God's holiness. King David wrote the following, "Sing praises to the LORD, you saints of His, and give thanks at the remembrance of His holy name" (Ps. 30:4).

God Called a Holy People

Throughout history, people have always acted like their gods. For example, if their god was a war god, they would be a warlike people. They would try to act like their god and please him by having lots of wars. This is how they worshiped their god. The more battles they won, the greater the worship. If their god was immoral, they would be immoral as an act of worship, and so forth. The highest form of worship is to imitate or act like your god.

In the midst of this confusion and worship of many false gods, the one true God revealed Himself so the world would know what He is like and imitate Him. And what did He say? "I am holy."

The ancient world inquired of God, "In what way are you holy?" God responded, "I'll show you My holiness through an entire nation of people who will worship Me. I'll be their holy

40

God, and they will be My holy people. When you see them, you'll see Me."

To implement His plan, God chose Abraham and his descendents as the nation of people through whom He would reveal His holiness to the world. God gave these words to Moses to give to the people, " 'Now therefore, if you will indeed obey My voice and keep My covenant, then you shall be a special treasure to Me above all people; for all the earth is Mine. And you shall be to Me a kingdom of priests and a holy nation.' These are the words which you shall speak to the children of Israel" (Ex. 19:5-6).

God instructed the Hebrews to be different from their pagan neighbors even as He was different from the pagan gods. The world would see God's holiness in His people. This revelation that God was holy would cause the people to turn from their evil ways and worship by imitating the one true God.

But for the most part, the Hebrews missed the real intent of God's holiness. They thought He was concerned only with their outward actions. While He was certainly interested in their behavior, He was primarily concerned with what was in their hearts.

God's ancient people began to add rule upon rule and regulation upon regulation to the basic laws God had given to them. They did not seem to understand that God was really desiring a holiness of the heart that would produce outward acts of holiness.

Jesus Is Holy

Finally, God determined to put His ultimate plan into effect. He clothed His holiness with flesh and blood, and became one of us. God prepared for Himself a body, in the person of Jesus Christ, and walked among us as a living example for the world

41

to see the true holiness of God. (See Colossians 2:9, 2 Corinthians 5:19 and Hebrews 10:5.)

At the time Jesus' birth was announced, the angel Gabriel declared Him to be the "Holy One of God" who was also the Son of God. Luke wrote, "And the angel answered and said to her, 'The Holy Spirit will come upon you, and the power of the Highest will overshadow you; therefore, also, that Holy One who is to be born will be called the Son of God'" (Luke 1:35).

Even demons recognized Jesus as the "Holy One of God." When Jesus went to Capernaum to preach, a man in the synagogue was demonized. The unclean demon in the man was afraid of Jesus and said to Him, " . . . Let us alone! What have we to do with You, Jesus of Nazareth? Did You come to destroy us? I know who You are — the Holy One of God! " (Luke 4:34)

As the holy Son of God, Jesus was different from the rest of us. He was the perfect revelation of the holiness of God. Through His words and life, Jesus taught us the true meaning of holiness, both in the heart and in outward deeds.

Jesus said to one of His disciples, " . . . He who has seen Me has seen the Father . . . " (John 14:9) Imitating the Father was His ultimate act of worship. As the people observed His life, they could see what God meant by "holy."

The Holy Spirit

Jesus showed us a way of life that is different from the world's standards. He also sent the Holy Spirit to help us live a holy life.

Jesus said, "If you then, being evil, know how to give good gifts to your children, how much more will your heavenly Father give the Holy Spirit to those who ask Him!" (Luke 11:13)

42

In Romans 1:4, Paul stated that we have received the "Spirit of holiness."

As we yield ourselves to God, the Holy Spirit will live the holy life of Jesus Christ in us, through us, and out of us. With the help of the Holy Spirit, we can imitate Jesus Christ, as our highest form of worship, so that the world can see His holy life in us.

Believers are Holy

Through our personal relationship with Jesus Christ, we are set apart from the world to God. Whatever God sets apart to Himself is considered to be holy by the very act of God setting it apart. God has prepared a body for His Spirit to live in. Believers who receive Christ into their lives are that body. (See 1 Corinthians 6:19-20.)

The Bible says:

Our God is holy (Lev. 19:2).
We have holy Scriptures (Rom. 1:2).
We have a holy covenant (Luke 1:72).
We have a holy calling (2 Tim. 1:9).
We are holy brethren (1 Thess. 5:27).
We are a holy priesthood (1 Pet. 2:5).
We are a holy nation (1 Pet. 2:9).
We are a holy temple (Eph. 2:21).
We have holy faith (Jude 20).
We worship with holy hands (1 Tim. 2:8).
We greet one another with a holy kiss (Rom. 16:16).
We will live forever in the holy city (Rev. 21:2).

This is the state of being or standing that all true believers have with God. He has separated us from the world and to Himself. This is what God has done for us. Now He desires to do the same thing in our everyday lives. He wants this holiness to be worked out, as an ongoing process, in our daily lives.

God does not seek to accomplish this through a legalistic code that religious people would try to use to control our behavior. He does not work through the rules and regulations, or the do's and don'ts of men. He works through the Holy Spirit, changing us into the likeness of Jesus Christ, so that His holy life is reproduced in us.

The Process of Holiness

There is a definite process by which God works His holiness in us. Paul gives us the key to this process in the following verses, "Therefore, my beloved, as you have always obeyed, not as in my presence only, but now much more in my absence, work out your own salvation with fear and trembling; for it is God who works in you both to will and to do for His good pleasure" (Phil. 2:12-13).

We learn from these verses that the process of holiness is a joint venture, a partnership between us and God. We can't do it without Him, and He won't do it without us.

Paul says that we must "work out our salvation." He does not say work for it, but work it out. We have a work or responsibility in this process, and so does the Holy Spirit.

One reason believers get so frustrated in this process is because they either try to accomplish holiness in their own strength, by following man's rules and regulations, or they expect the Holy Spirit to accomplish it for them, without their participation. Both the Holy Spirit and the believer have a responsibility in this process.

We will never develop a holy life without the help of the Holy Spirit. But neither will He do all of the work for us. It's a partnership; the believer and the Holy Spirit each has his own work to accomplish.

Let's now see how this partnership develops, so we can

44

better understand what God is responsible to do, and what we must do.

A chart entitled "The Process of Holiness" is provided at the end of this chapter. In this chart, I explain how God and the believer work together to produce true holiness in our lives. You should refer to this chart as you read the following explanation.

Notice that the chart is divided into two columns entitled, "God's Part" and "Believer's Part." Then the six steps in the process of holiness are listed. God's responsibilities are shown on the left and the believer's on the right. Let's begin our explanation with God's part.

God Draws Near to Us

God is the One who initiates this process in our lives. He promises to draw near to us. James wrote, "Draw near to God and He will draw near to you . . . " (James 4:8) God desires to have an intimate, personal relationship with us. He wants to share His life with us and manifest His presence to us. But we must respond.

We Present Our Bodies

God will draw near to us as we draw near to Him. How do we draw near to God? We draw near to God by presenting our bodies to Him. Paul wrote, "I beseech you therefore, brethren, by the mercies of God, that you present your bodies a living sacrifice, holy, acceptable to God, which is your reasonable service" (Rom. 12:1).

If you are a believer, God has chosen to live inside your body so that He may have fellowship with you, and you with Him. He has purchased your body by giving the body of His own Son on the cross. We, therefore, must no longer live for ourselves, but for Him.

Every choice we make concerning our bodies should be made with the following thought in mind, "Or do you not know that your body is the temple of the Holy Spirit who is in you, whom you have from God, and you are not your own? For you were bought at a price; therefore glorify God in your body and in your spirit, which are God's" (1 Cor. 6:19-20).

Because God lives in us, we are to use our bodies in such a way that He is glorified in them. This means that we must discipline our bodies. Paul wrote of this need in his own life and said, "But I discipline my body and bring it into subjection . . . " (1 Cor. 9:27)

It is certainly not easy to discipline our bodies. But God will draw near to us and help us. One of the obvious areas in which we need to discipline our bodies is moral purity. We must not subject our bodies to immorality or any type of television programming, movies, videos, reading material, or filthy conversation or acts that would stimulate the lust of the flesh.

A second way we present our bodies is by the way we dress. Peter wrote the following to Christian women, "Do not let your adornment be merely outward — arranging the hair, wearing gold, or putting on fine apparel — rather let it be the hidden person of the heart, with the incorruptible [imperishable] beauty of a gentle and quiet spirit, which is very precious in the sight of God" (1 Pet. 3:3-4).

Although Peter's words were written directly to women, it is also important for Christian men to dress modestly, not calling attention to themselves or giving the impression that they are inordinately following the fashions of the world.

We should also be very careful about what we put into our bodies. The American public is just beginning to realize the direct relationship between our health and the kinds of food we eat. Even though we have plenty of food in America, our bodies are starving for quality food that contains the ingredients necessary to keep our bodies healthy.

We need to be aware of both the quality and quantity of food we eat, and make whatever adjustments are necessary so that God is glorified in our bodies. And we certainly would not want to put alcohol, tobacco, drugs or any other harmful chemical substance into our bodies, because the Holy Spirit lives in them along with us.

Another way of presenting our bodies to God is through a modest exercise program and proper rest. We need to exercise our bodies to make them strong and healthy. Some type of physical activity is vital to keep our bodies functioning properly. And a good night's sleep is necessary to refresh and renew our bodies so that we can use them for God's glory.

God Renews Our Minds

The first step in the process of holiness relates to our bodies. The next three deal with our souls, which consist of our minds, our emotions and our wills.

God is responsible to renew our minds. After Paul wrote about presenting our bodies, he stated we must be transformed by the renewing of our minds. He said, "And do not be conformed to this world, but be transformed by the renewing of your mind, that you may prove what is that good and acceptable and perfect will of God" (Rom. 12:2).

Why does God want to renew our minds? Because we don't think like He does. God expressed it this way through Isaiah, "For My thoughts are not your thoughts, nor are your ways My ways . . . For as the heavens are higher than the earth, so are My ways higher than your ways, and My thoughts than your thoughts" (Isa. 55:8-9).

We Meditate on Scripture

In order for God to renew our minds, we must meditate on His Word. Joshua 1:8 reads, "This Book of the Law shall not depart from your mouth, but you shall meditate in it day and night, that you may observe to do according to all that is written in it . . ."

King David understood the necessity of meditating on God's Word and wrote, "I will meditate on Your precepts, and contemplate Your ways. I will delight myself in Your statutes; I will not forget Your word" (Ps. 119:15-16).

When we meditate on God's Word, the Holy Spirit renews our minds with the mind of Christ so that we will think like God and be filled with His thoughts. (See 1 Corinthians 2:9-16.) But the Holy Spirit will not do this unless we cooperate by diligently meditating on God's Word. If you need help in this area, may I suggest you read my book *Come and Dine*, which is available through this ministry.

God Convicts Our Emotions

The third responsibility from God is to convict our emotions. Jesus spoke of this work of the Holy Spirit with these words, "Nevertheless I tell you the truth. It is to your advantage that I go away; for if I do not go away, the Helper will not come to you; but if I depart, I will send Him to you. And when He has come, He will convict the world of sin, and of righteousness, and of judgement" (John 16:7-8).

It is necessary for God to convict our emotions because sin blinds us spiritually, dulling our minds and hardening our hearts. Without His help, we would be unaware of the need to repent.

We Set Our Affections

We can cooperate with the Holy Spirit by setting our

affections on the things of God. Paul wrote these words, "Set your affection on things above, not on things on the earth" (Col. 3:2, KJV).

When we focus our thoughts and emotions on God, the Holy Spirit convicts us about attitudes and habits that are not pleasing to God. As we become more God conscious, we will lay aside our emotional attachment to sin and seek the things of God.

God Empowers Our Wills

It is also God's responsibility to empower our wills so that we are able to respond to His prompting. We may desire to do God's will in our minds and emotions, but find that we just don't have the power. So we fail!

Paul experienced these failures many times in his own life before learning to rely on the Holy Spirit. He wrote the following words for our encouragement, "I say then: Walk in the Spirit, and you shall not fulfill the lust of the flesh" (Gal. 5:16).

We Submit Our Wills

It is wonderful to know that God is ready and able to help us obey Him. But we must cooperate! We cooperate by submitting our wills to Him. James wrote, "Therefore submit to God . . . " (James 4:7)

As we submit our wills to God, the Holy Spirit empowers and energizes us so that we can do God's will. This is more than just a one-time experience with the Holy Spirit. It is a way of life as we daily yield ourselves to God and ask the Holy Spirit to completely fill our souls with His divine presence.

God Provides a Way of Escape

The first four steps in the process of holiness relate to our bodies and souls. The next two work in our spirits. God promises to help us overcome temptation and to provide a means for us to escape its snares.

Paul said it this way, "No temptation has overtaken you except such as is common to man; but God is faithful, who will not allow you to be tempted beyond what you are able, but with the temptation will also make the way of escape, that you may be able to bear it" (1 Cor. 10:13).

We Flee Temptation

Now what is our part? Our part simply is to flee temptation. Paul wrote these words for our instruction, "Flee sexual immorality . . . " (1 Cor. 6:18) To the same group of believers he said, " . . . flee from idolatry" (1 Cor. 10:14).

He gave the following word to Timothy regarding greed, "But you, O man of God, flee these things and pursue righteousness, godliness, faith, love, patience, gentleness" (1 Tim. 6:11).

He wrote again to Timothy, "Flee also youthful lusts; but pursue righteousness, faith, love, peace with those who call on the Lord out of a pure heart" (2 Tim. 2:22).

The practical way we flee temptation is by simply refusing to go anywhere, do anything, or hang around with anyone where we will be vulnerable to temptation. When we do our part, God will be faithful to help us resist temptations and give us deliverance.

God Causes Us to Triumph

Finally, God will make sure that we are victorious. Paul encourages us with these words, "Now thanks be to God who always leads [causes] us to triumph in Christ . . . " (2 Cor. 2:14)

Christians do not have to yield to temptation nor must they be oppressed by Satan. God has done all that is required to give us victory through the Lord Jesus Christ. As Paul so boldly declared to the believers in Rome, "For sin shall not have dominion over you . . . " (Rom. 6:14)

John said it this way, "You are of God, little children, and have overcome them, because He who is in you is greater than he who is in the world" (1 John 4:4).

We Resist the Devil

God has given us the Holy Spirit to help us live a holy life. But He won't do it for us if we're just passive. We have to actively cooperate by resisting Satan. James wrote, " . . . Resist the devil and he will flee from you" (James 4:7).

But how do we resist Satan? We resist him by presenting our bodies to God, by meditating on Scripture, by setting our affections on things above, by submitting our will to God and by fleeing temptation.

God is ready and able to help us live a holy life. He has given us the Holy Spirit so that we can live a holy life. Because of what God has done for us, we must respond. Paul encourages us with these words, "Therefore, having these promises, beloved, let us cleanse ourselves from all filthiness of the flesh and spirit, perfecting holiness in the fear of God" (2 Cor. 7:1).

Seeing God's Glory

The writer of the book of Hebrews tells us how we can see the glory of God and experience revival in our lives. He said, "Pursue peace with all people, and holiness, without which no one will see the Lord" (Heb. 12:14).

The word "see" used in this verse means much more than just casually observing or looking upon at a distance. It means to gaze at with wide-open eyes. It is a close-at-hand inspection. It is the type of inspection requiring a zoom lens or a magnifying glass in order to see the full beauty and detail of your object. The full meaning of the word is to "experience."

This word is used in Luke 2:26 concerning the promise God gave to Simeon that he would not "see" death until he saw the Messiah. It is used in the same way in Hebrews 11:5 regarding Enoch, who was taken away so he did not "see" death.

As we discover the full meaning of this word, we realize the profound truth it teaches: no one will have a visitation from God and experience personal revival without holiness.

THE PROCESS OF HOLINESS

GOD'S PART	BELIEVER'S PART
DRAW NEAR TO US	PRESENT OUR BODIES
RENEW OUR MINDS	MEDITATE ON SCRIPTURE
CONVICT OUR EMOTIONS	SET OUR AFFECTIONS
EMPOWER OUR WILLS	SUBMIT OUR WILLS
PROVIDE WAY OF ESCAPE	FLEE TEMPTATION
CAUSE US TO TRIUMPH	RESIST THE DEVIL

Chapter 4 — Walking the Highway of Holiness
Study Guide 4

1. What does it mean to he holy?

2. Why is it necessary to be holy?

3. Explain the process of holiness, including how we cooperate with God to "work out our salvation."

4. Ask God to show you areas in your life where you need to cooperate with Him in developing personal holiness.

5

Praying Fervently

Prayer is one of the most important prerequisites of revival and a visitation from God. To the best of my knowledge, there has never been a revival in the history of God's people unless it was preceded by prayer. And the coming revival will be ushered in through the earnest prayers of God's people.

The apostle James spoke of the necessity and power of prayer with these words: " . . . The effective, fervent prayer of a righteous man avails much" (James 5:16).

James used the word "fervent" to describe the type or intensity of prayer that is required of us before God will make Himself known. The word means heated to the point of boiling. In regard to prayer, it is a white-hot zeal for the glory of God that burns within our hearts and drives us to our knees.

We call this type of praying "intercessory prayer," and we are going to discuss it in this chapter.

The Purpose of Intercessory Prayer

In intercessory prayer, we express our concern for the glory of God and the needs of others. This is perhaps the most important type of prayer mentioned in the Bible. When Paul wrote to Timothy, he mentioned prayer as the top priority for Timothy's life. Here's how he said it, "Therefore I exhort first of all that supplications, prayers, intercessions, and giving of thanks be made for all men" (1 Tim. 2:1).

The basic purpose of intercessory prayer is to act as an intermediary between God and man on behalf of others so that the will of God can be accomplished on earth as it is in heaven (Matt. 6:10).

The prophet Isaiah ministered during a time of great sin in Israel. God desired to spare the people from judgement and held back His holy anger until intercessors could begin to pray for the people. But as time passed, no one interceded. Finally, Isaiah spoke these words to the people concerning God, "He saw that there was no man, and wondered that there was no intercessor . . . " (Isa. 59:16)

Apparently the Hebrews failed to understand how important this was to God. As time passed, He spoke to this problem again through the prophet Ezekiel. He said, "So I sought for a man among them who would make a wall, and stand in the gap before Me on behalf of the land, that I should not destroy it; but I found no one. Therefore I have poured out My indignation on them; I have consumed them with the fire of My wrath . . . " (Ezek. 22:30-31)

Abraham and Sodom

There are many great examples of intercessory prayer mentioned in the Bible. Let's begin with Abraham.

Around the year 2000 B.C., God appeared to Abraham and told Abraham of His plans to destroy the wicked cities of Sodom and Gomorrah. This troubled Abraham greatly, so he began to intercede with God on behalf of the people. Abraham asked God, " . . . Would You also destroy the righteous with the wicked?" (Gen. 18:23)

Abraham then began to bargain with God. He asked God to spare the city if just fifty righteous people could be found. God agreed! Abraham must have given a big sigh of relief and somehow found the courage to bargain even harder. He asked God to spare the city if just forty-five righteous could be found. Then forty, thirty, twenty and ten. Each time God agreed.

Unfortunately, God could not find even ten righteous people in the towns of Sodom and Gomorrah, so He had to destroy them by fire after allowing Lot and his family to escape.

We learn from this story that one intercessor can make the difference in the destiny of an entire city. I'm sure the city council at Sodom was busy making plans for the many wicked activities they would promote in the city during the next months. But the future of the city was not in their hands. It was in the hands of one man who had access to God.

The news media often talks about the power of government and the politicians who seem to run the country. But the most powerful people on earth are not the politicians. The most powerful people on earth are the intercessors, because they have access to God, who rules over the nations.

I have discovered through my study of the Bible and secular history, as well as from personal experience, that world powers rise and fall as the people of God rise and fall to their knees. You can make a difference in your family, your community, your state, your country and even world events through fervent intercessory prayer.

As former President Reagan expressed it, "Let us also reflect that in the prayers of simple people there is more power and might than that possessed by all the great statesmen or armies of the earth" (Address to the Nation, December 10, 1987).

Moses at Sinai

Our next example of intercession took place around 1500 B.C. While Moses was having his mountaintop experience with God, the children of Israel were down below worshiping a golden calf. They must have had a short memory because they gave the golden calf credit for delivering them from Egypt.

Needless to say, God was not pleased with this memory lapse. After letting Moses in on what was happening below, He threatened to destroy the Hebrews and start again with Moses.

Moses was greatly distressed and began to intercede on behalf of the people. We read in Exodus, "Then Moses pleaded with the LORD his God, and said: 'LORD, why does Your wrath burn hot against Your people whom You have brought out of the land of Egypt with great power and with a mighty hand? Why should the Egyptians speak, and say, "He brought them out to harm them, to kill them in the mountains, and to consume them from the face of the earth"? Turn from Your fierce wrath, and relent from this harm to Your people. Remember Abraham, Isaac, and Israel, Your servants, to whom You swore by Your own self, and said to them, "I will multiply your descendants as the stars of the heaven; and all this land that I have spoken of I give to your descendants, and they shall inherit it forever." ' So the LORD relented from the harm which He said He would do to His people" (Ex. 32:11-14).

We all have family members and friends who, like the children of Israel, have golden calves in their lives. They are not literal golden calves, but anything that people put ahead of God. This is certainly a concern to God and should be to us as well. You can postpone God's judgement on their sins, and give them further time to repent, by pleading for God's mercy through intercessory prayer.

Peter's Great Escape

One of the most powerful, yet humorous, examples of

intercessory prayer is recorded in the book of Acts. Here's what happened.

King Herod arrested Peter during the week of Passover and placed him under the guard of sixteen soldiers. Herod intended to execute Peter, who was double-chained between two of the guards the night before he was to be killed.

When word reached the believers in Jerusalem about Peter's imprisonment and imminent death, they began to pray. Luke wrote, "Peter was therefore kept in prison, but constant [earnest] prayer was offered to God for him by the church" (Acts 12:5).

God heard their prayers and sent an angel to deliver Peter, who was asleep when the angel appeared. The angel gave Peter a "holy slap" to awaken him and escorted him safely past the guards and outside the prison gate.

Peter was unsure what was taking place and thought his great escape was just a dream or vision. But once he was outside the prison gate and walking the street, he realized that God had sent an angel to deliver him, and that he was now free.

When he came to his senses, he went to the house where the believers were praying and knocked at the door. Luke wrote, "So, when he had considered this, he came to the house of Mary, the mother of John whose surname was Mark, where many were gathered together praying" (Acts 12:12). A young girl named Rhoda came to answer the door, and when she realized it was Peter, she was overcome with joy and shouted the good news to everyone.

But these great prayer warriors didn't believe her. Instead of going to the door to see for themselves, they continued to ask God to deliver Peter from prison and spare his life.

Finally, at the girl's insistence, they stopped praying long enough to go to the door. When they realized it truly was Peter, they quickly let him into the house. After he told them what had happened, they sent him to a safer location. (See Acts 12:1-19.)

Peter was in a literal prison. But there are many who are in spiritual prisons. They are bound up with chains of oppression, depression, fear, poverty, disease, sin and rebellion. Satan desires to take their lives, and he has assigned his demon soldiers to guard them. Your earnest intercession can set them free as did the prayers of the believers on behalf of Peter.

The Perfect Intercessor

There are many other examples in the Bible, and history, of ordinary men and women whose intercession changed the course of world events. But the greatest intercessor of all times is Jesus Christ.

The writer of Hebrews tells us why Jesus is the perfect intercessor we all need. He wrote, "But He [Jesus], because He continues forever, has an unchangeable priesthood. Therefore He is able to save to the uttermost [completely or forever] those who come to God through Him, since He always lives to make intercession for them" (Heb. 7:24-25).

In the ancient world, people turned away from God and no longer knew Him. But God is merciful and desired to make Himself known. The way He did this was to choose the descendants of Abraham as the ethnic people through which He would reveal Himself to the nations.

God selected a particular family to be the priests who would intercede for the nation of Israel. Aaron was the first High Priest. At his death, he was succeeded by his oldest son. This way the priesthood would be passed down from generation to generation. (See Exodus 28-29 and Leviticus 8.)

But Aaron and his sons were imperfect just like all the rest of us. They had imperfect animal sacrifices to offer to God. Therefore, the job of the High Priest was never finished. He had to keep offering the same sacrifices year after year, for his own sins and the sins of the people. As soon as he got good at being a priest, he would die. Yet God, in His grace, accepted the High Priest as the intercessor for the people until one greater than Aaron would come along.

This "Greater One" is the Lord Jesus Christ! He was God in human flesh, who laid aside His own glory to be our once-and-for-all sacrifice. He humbled Himself and died on the cross, taking the consequences of our sins in His spirit, our sorrows in His soul, and our sickness and diseases in His flesh. (See Philippians 2:9-11.)

Isaiah explained it this way, "Surely He has borne our griefs and carried our sorrows; yet we esteemed Him stricken, smitten by God and afflicted. But He was wounded for our transgressions, He was bruised for our iniquities; the chastisement of our peace was upon Him, and by His stripes we are healed" (Isa. 53:4-5).

Jesus became the ultimate intercessor when He who knew no sin became sin for us on the cross (2 Cor. 5:21). But death and the grave could not hold Him. He was raised on the third day and returned to heaven, to minister at the right hand of God on our behalf.

We have been forgiven and made whole, once and for all, by the blood of Jesus Christ. He is the perfect sacrifice. His shed blood accomplished what the blood of animals could never do. His blood didn't just cover our sins; it took them away to be remembered no more. Therefore Jesus doesn't offer Himself again and again like the High Priest who continually offered the animals.

Unlike the High Priest of ancient times, Jesus lives forever. Therefore, He is always there to take our concerns to God and intercede on our behalf. He is exactly the kind of High Priest we need.

In view of this, Paul wrote, "Be anxious for nothing, but in everything by prayer and supplication, with thanksgiving, let your requests be made known to God; and the peace of God, which surpasses all understanding, will guard your hearts and minds through Christ Jesus" (Phil. 4:6-7).

Peter wrote the following words of encouragement, "Cast all your anxieties [cares] on him, for he cares for you" (1 Pet. 5:7, RSV).

Principles of Intercession

It's wonderful to know that God cares for us and has provided the ministry of intercession for us and to us through Jesus Christ. It's exciting to realize that we can have such a profound influence on people and events through fervent prayer. But how do we actually pray a powerful prayer of intercession?

There are seven basic principles to guide us in making our intercession effective. Let's now consider each of them for the purpose of learning how to apply them to our lives.

1. Burdened by God to Pray

The first principle is that the intercessor is burdened by God to pray. In about the year 425 B.C., God spoke to a man named Malachi and stirred his heart for the people of Israel that they might return to God.

Here's the way the Bible expresses it, "The burden of the word of the LORD to Israel by Malachi" (Mal. 1:1).

Malachi spoke of the "burden of the Word of the Lord." What did he mean by this? The burden of the Word of the

62

Lord is an overwhelming concern for God's glory, God's plans, God's purposes and God's people to be established on the earth. It is more than just a casual concern or passing interest.

This is a God-initiated fire that burns in your heart. It is a holy zeal for the things of God to be manifested in a specific area of concern to God which He has put in your heart.

The Bible says if you will draw near to God, He will draw near to you and reveal to you those things that concern Him on the earth. (See James 4:8 and Psalm 25:14.)

God takes a particular burden or concern that is on His heart and transfers it to your heart. It's now in His heart and yours. His burden becomes your burden. His concern becomes your concern. You become God's prayer partner, interceding with Jesus Christ for God's will to be manifested in a special or specific way on the earth. The burden will not be lifted, and you will not stop interceding, until you see the prayer answered.

2. Clean on the Inside

In order for us to be effective as intercessors, we must have clean hearts and no unconfessed sin.

When King David sinned, his fellowship with God was broken. This caused him much sadness and grief. His greatest desire was to be restored to God.

David cried out to God, "Have mercy upon me, O God, according to Your lovingkindness; according to the multitude of Your tender mercies, blot out my transgressions. Wash me thoroughly from my iniquity, and cleanse me from my sin. Create in me a clean heart, O God, and renew a steadfast [right] spirit within me. Do not cast me away from Your presence, and do not take Your Holy Spirit from me" (Ps. 51:1-2,10-11).

Although David was just a man and made many mistakes, he desired God's presence above everything else in his life. In fact, the Bible gives the highest commendation to David. It says he was a man after God's own heart (Acts 13:22).

As intercessors, we must have such hearts for God that we will desire to be morally pure and without blame. We must be so concerned for the glory of God and His redemptive purposes that we will make sure there is nothing within us that would hinder the burden of the Word of the Lord from being accomplished. And if we discover something in our lives that is not pleasing to God, we will quickly turn from it.

James gives a hard word that many will not receive; but intercessors will, because they know how necessary it is for their walk with God. James wrote: "Draw near to God and He will draw near to you. Cleanse your hands, you sinners; and purify your hearts, you double-minded. Lament and mourn and weep! Let your laughter be turned to mourning and your joy to gloom. Humble yourselves in the sight of the Lord, and He will lift you up" (James 4:8-10).

3. Not Concerned with Personal Needs

One stumbling block to many people that keeps them from God is their desire for personal comfort, security and possessions. They will serve God if it's convenient and not too costly.

But the intercessor is different. Intercessors are not concerned about personal comforts. They will make any sacrifice necessary in order to see the burden of the Word of God fulfilled.

The prophet Ezekiel is an extreme example of this. Because of Israel's sin, God allowed the Babylonian armies to invade and conquer the land. As a way of warning the people, God called Ezekiel to prophesy about the coming destruction of Jerusalem.

Not only did Ezekiel prophesy about the coming invasion, he also had to act out his words so the people could have a visual aid of what was going to happen. (See Ezekiel 4-5.)

God required Ezekiel to lie on his left side, one day for each year that the northern kingdom of Israel would be in captivity. Then God required Ezekiel to lie on his right side, one day for each year that the southern Kingdom of Israel would be in captivity.

During this time, Ezekiel was limited to one meal a day. This "meal" consisted of eight ounces of defiled bread and one quart of water. The purpose of Ezekiel's plight was to dramatically illustrate to the people the rationing of bread and water which would occur during the siege of Jerusalem, because only small amounts would be available.

Furthermore, God instructed Ezekiel to shave his head and beard, and weigh it into three equal parts. He was to burn a third, slash another third with his knife, and scatter the last third to the wind. This was God's way of showing the people their fate: one-third would die from famine and disease, one-third would be killed by the enemy, and one-third would be scattered.

This was certainly not a pleasant experience for Ezekiel. But he was willing to do whatever was required to warn the people, with the hope that they would turn from their sins.

We learn from this example that the true intercessor is willing to pay any price to see the burden of the Word of God manifested. It is the intercessor's primary reason for living and the focus of his life. It sets the course and direction of his life. He becomes single-minded and will do whatever is required to bring it to fulfillment. Personal needs and creature comforts are not even a consideration for one whose heart has been burdened with the Word of the Lord.

Jesus expressed this attitude when He said, "My food is to do the will of Him who sent Me, and to finish His work" (John 4:34).

4. Conducts Spiritual Warfare

The intercessor is like the front-line foot soldier in the war against Satan. Intercessors conduct spiritual warfare on behalf of others.

The Pharisees were jealous of Jesus and confused as to who He was and what He was doing. On one occasion when Jesus cast demons out of a man, the Pharisees accused Him of getting His power from Satan.

Jesus showed the foolishness of this accusation and then spoke about the necessity of binding Satan, who He referred to as the strong man. Matthew recorded these words from Jesus, "Or else how can one enter a strong man's house and plunder his goods, unless he first binds the strong man? And then he will plunder his house" (Matt. 12:29).

It seems that Satan has assigned ruling spirits to carry out his commands over the nations for the purpose of bringing humanity under his authority and control. (See Ephesians 6:10-12.) These ruling spirits seek to establish strongholds over all structures of society, including the government (national and local), the media, educational organizations, recreational and leisure activities, religious organizations (including local churches) and even families, which he attacks through familiar spirits.

Intercessors conduct spiritual warfare by identifying and binding these powers of darkness and by loosing the power of God.

Jesus spoke of this ministry of the intercessor with these words, "And I will give you the keys of the kingdom of heaven, and whatever you bind on earth will be bound in heaven, and whatever you loose on earth will be loosed in heaven" (Matt. 16:19).

A casual reading of this text seems to indicate that the binding and loosing will take place in the future. To our way of thinking, the phrases "will give" and "will be" speak of something that will happen in the future.

But when this Scripture was written in the original language, the phrases were in the past tense. We would write it today as, "I have given you the keys of the kingdom of heaven, and whatever you bind on earth has already been bound in heaven, and whatever you loose on earth has already been loosed in heaven."

This means that from eternity past, God has purposed within Himself to establish His plan of redemption on the earth and has made available every provision to us so that we might pray it into being. We simply decree His will to be done and, through our intercession, both bind the forces of evil that would hinder it and loose God's redemptive power and grace.

Paul stated it this way, "For though we walk in the flesh, we do not war according to the flesh. For the weapons of our warfare are not carnal but mighty in God for pulling down strongholds, casting down arguments and every high thing that exalts itself against the knowledge of God, bringing every thought into captivity to the obedience of Christ" (2 Cor. 10:3-5).

5. Identifies with Others

One challenging aspect of intercession is the need to identify with those for whom we are interceding. This is necessary in order for us to fully relate to the needs of the people and the circumstances for which we are praying.

The Bible teaches that because He became one of us, God is able to relate to all the needs and hurts of humanity. The writer of Hebrews said, "Inasmuch then as the children have partaken of flesh and blood, He Himself likewise shared in the same, that through death He might destroy him who had the power of death, that is, the devil" (Heb. 2:14).

You know, it is very easy to give money to a visiting missionary who may be preaching in a Sunday service at our Church. No effort is required to put a few dollars in the collection plate as it is being passed. But it requires a real sacrifice to spend our vacation with the missionary, eating what he eats, sleeping where he sleeps, living in the conditions where he lives, and sharing his problems and circumstances.

After sharing his life, we are better able to identify with the missionary's needs and fully relate to his situation. And I'm sure we would be much more generous with our offering the next time the collection plate was passed for him.

6. Listens and Declares

Another important principle of intercession is that the one interceding listens to God's voice and speaks or declares what God says. This means we must listen to God's voice during the time of intercession. Instead of doing all the talking ourselves, we should have a time of silent waiting for God to speak.

Jesus said, "My sheep hear My voice . . . " (John 10:27). The best time to hear His voice is during times of intercession.

We learned previously from the writer of Hebrews that Jesus is at the right hand of God making intercession for us

(Heb. 7:24-25). He is our intercessor in heaven, who knows the mind of God and His perfect will. He is able to communicate this to us through the Holy Spirit, who is our intercessor on earth.

The Holy Spirit lives in all believers. He is the link between heaven and earth. He alone on the earth knows the prayer of Jesus in heaven, and He speaks it to our hearts and minds when we listen for His voice.

Here's how Paul stated it: " 'Eye has not seen, nor ear heard, nor have entered into the heart of man the things which God has prepared for those who love Him.' But God has revealed them to us through His Spirit. For the Spirit searches all things, yes, the deep things of God. For what man knows the things of a man except the spirit of the man which is in him? Even so no one knows the things of God except the Spirit of God. Now we have received, not the spirit of the world, but the Spirit who is from God, that we might know the things that have been fully given to us by God" (1 Cor. 2:9-12).

The Holy Spirit intercedes for us and through us, helping us to know the mind of Christ so that His prayer in heaven becomes our prayer on earth. We then speak or declare this revealed will of God so that it might be manifested on the earth.

Paul further explained with these words, "Likewise the Spirit also helps us in our weaknesses. For we do not know what we should pray for as we ought, but the Spirit Himself makes intercession for us with groanings which cannot be uttered. Now He who searches the hearts knows what the mind of the Spirit is, because He makes intercession for the saints according to the will of God" (Rom. 8:26-27).

7. Meets the Need

Finally, the intercessor meets the prayer need wherever it is possible and wise to do so.

God created us in His image and after His likeness so that we could know Him and have fellowship with Him. When Adam and Eve sinned, man's fellowship with God was broken. This grieved God. But because He loves us, God did something about the situation. He sent His Son to die for our sins so that we might be reconciled to Him.

The Bible says, "For God so loved the world that He gave His only begotten Son, that whoever believes in Him should not perish but have everlasting life" (John 3:16).

If we can do something to help a person or change a situation, action is required, not prayer! If we can be the answer to our own prayer, we don't need to pray; we need to act with love and wisdom.

For example, if a hard-working Christian friend loses his or her job and can't pay the bills, we don't need to grab the person's hand and ask God to help the person. Instead, we should grab our checkbooks and pay the person's bills.

The Bible puts it this way, "By this we know love, because He laid down His life for us. And we also ought to lay down our lives for the brethren. But whoever has this world's goods, and sees his brother in need, and shuts up his heart from him, how does the love of God abide in him? My little children, let us not love in word or in tongue, but in deed and in truth" (1 John 3:16-18).

I hope that through this discussion you can see the necessity of intercessory prayer and the importance of your role as a prayer partner with God. I encourage you to commit yourself to this vital, dynamic ministry so that you can help change the world. Ask God to show you what He thinks is important. Ask

Him to ignite your heart with a fire that cannot be quenched. Ask Him to give you a burden for revival. Ask Him to give you a holy zeal for His glory, His plans, His purposes and His people. And may God bless you as you labor to bring the burden of the Word of the Lord from heaven to earth.

Chapter 5 — Praying Fervently
Study Guide 5

1. What is the primary purpose of intercessory prayer?

2. State four examples of intercession recorded in the Bible.

3. List the seven principles of intercession and determine how each can apply to your life.

4. Ask God to give you a burden for the things that concern Him about your family, Church, community, etc. Then find some people who share that burden and become active in an intercessory prayer group. Seek to identify the specific strongholds that are hindering the work of God and pull them down so that revival can come to your area with a time of refreshing from the presence of the Lord.

6

Fasting in Faith

Fervent praying is often accompanied by one of the most important disciplines practiced by Christians down through the ages. Yet, it is one of the most neglected in our modern times. This is the biblically-sanctioned practice of fasting.

Fasting is certainly not a normal part of life in our western, pleasure-seeking, self-gratifying society. When it is brought to our attention, we generally think of it as an antiquated custom, which is sometimes practiced by people we tend to view as a bit radical in their thinking.

Yet, you may be surprised to know that fasting was a required part of Jewish religious life, as well as a common practice in the lives of Jesus, first-century believers, and both Christians and non-Christians throughout history.

Fasting has always had a significant role as a spiritual discipline that precedes revival, and the revelation and manifestation of the glory of God. For this reason, it is important for us to gain an understanding of fasting and how we can practice it as an act of faith in preparing for the coming revival.

What is Fasting?

The most basic definition of biblical fasting is to abstain from food and/or drink for religious purposes. Biblical fasting

73

relates to spiritual matters and is usually practiced when our concern for God's interests requires a more intense level of commitment and preparation than normal. Fasting is usually practiced temporarily for a pre-determined length of time, although many people do fast on a regular basis.

The Purpose of Fasting

The purpose of fasting is to concentrate our attention on moral and spiritual concerns as a higher priority in our life than fleshly appetites. It necessarily involves self-denial.

Of course, self does not like to be denied. But when we are burdened with the Word of the Lord, our concern and zeal for the things of God become a stronger motivation to us than our desire for food.

The prophet Isaiah wrote the classic chapter in the Bible on fasting. (See Isaiah 58.) I suggest that you take the time to read this entire chapter. In the key verse of the chapter, God spoke through Isaiah and said, "Is this not the fast that I have chosen: to loose the bonds of wickedness, to undo the heavy burdens, to let the oppressed go free, and that you break every yoke?" (Isa. 58:6) Here we discover the true purpose of fasting.

We learn from the pen of Isaiah that fasting is a means to an end. The end is to bring moral and spiritual renewal with the result being that God is glorified and people are set free from sin and demonic oppression. Perhaps this is why Satan has blinded our eyes to the importance of fasting as a spiritual weapon.

Fasting in the Old Testament

The Bible has much to say about fasting. The word "fast" in its various forms is mentioned approximately 78 times. In addition, the biblical phrase "afflict your souls" involved a humbling of the people before God that always included fasting.

God established the Jewish Day of Atonement as a national day of "soul affliction" which included fasting. (See Leviticus 16:29-31 and 23:27-32.)

Moses fasted forty days and nights when he received the commandments from God. He continued this another forty days and nights while he interceded for the people after they sinned by making the golden calf idol. (See Exodus 34:28 and Deuteronomy 9:18.)

King David fasted for the life of his firstborn. We read in the book of Samuel, "David therefore pleaded with God for the child, and David fasted and went in and lay all night on the ground" (2 Sam. 12:16).

David must have fasted frequently. He wrote these words, " . . . I humbled myself with fasting . . . " (Ps. 35:13) In Psalm 69:10 he said, "When I wept and chastened my soul with fasting . . . " And another time he wrote, "My knees are weak through fasting, and my flesh is feeble from lack of fatness" (Ps. 109:24).

Ezra fasted for protection when leading a group of exiles back from Babylon to Jerusalem. He wrote, "Then I proclaimed a fast there at the river of Ahava, that we might humble ourselves before our God, to seek from Him the right way for us and our little ones and all our possessions. So we fasted and entreated our God for this, and He answered our prayer" (Ezra 8:21,23).

When Nehemiah heard the sad news of the state of affairs in Jerusalem, he was overcome with grief and fasted to God for help. He wrote, "So it was, when I heard these words, that I sat down and wept, and mourned for many days; I was fasting and praying before the God of heaven" (Neh. 1:4).

During one of the greatest crises in the history of Israel, God raised up Esther to intercede for her people. The key to her success was prayer and fasting. When the king decreed that all Jews were to be killed, they fasted for deliverance. We learn from the book of Esther, "And in every province where the king's command and decree arrived, there was great mourning among the Jews, with fasting, weeping and wailing; and many lay in sackcloth and ashes" (Esther 4:3).

Esther decided to enter the king's court without permission, seeking to help her people. She instructed her aides, "Go, gather all the Jews who are present in Shushan, and fast for me; neither eat nor drink for three days, night or day. My maids and I will fast likewise . . . " (Esther 4:16)

The prophet Daniel fasted when seeking to understand the Word of God concerning the captivity of the Jews in Babylon. We read in Daniel: "Then I set my face toward the Lord God to make request by prayer and supplications, with fasting, sackcloth, and ashes" (Dan. 9:3).

Three times the prophet Joel called for fasting as a means of seeking God. Joel wrote, "Consecrate a fast, call a sacred assembly; gather the elders and all the inhabitants of the land into the house of the LORD your God, and cry out to the LORD" (Joel 1:14).

In the following chapter he wrote these words on behalf of God, " 'Now, therefore,' says the LORD, 'Turn to Me with all your heart, with fasting, with weeping, and with mourning.' Blow the trumpet in Zion, consecrate a fast, call a sacred assembly" (Joel 2:12,15).

When Jonah preached at Nineveh, the people repented and fasted: "So the people of Nineveh believed God, proclaimed a fast, and put on sackcloth, from the greatest to the least of them" (Jon. 3:5).

Fasting in the New Testament
In the New Testament, we learn that Jesus fasted on one

76

occasion for forty days and nights. Matthew wrote, "And when He had fasted forty days and forty nights, afterward He was hungry" (Matt. 4:2).

John the Baptist and his followers also practiced fasting. We learn this from Matthew 9:14 when one of John's disciples came to Jesus with the following question: " . . . Why do we and the Pharisees fast often, but Your disciples do not fast?" Although Jesus' disciples did not fast while they were with Him, they did fast after He returned to heaven.

Believers in the early church also practiced fasting. It was during such a time that God spoke to them about the establishing of local Churches. Luke wrote, "As they ministered to the Lord and fasted, the Holy Spirit said, 'Now separate to Me Barnabas and Saul for the work to which I have called them' " (Acts 13:2).

Paul certainly learned from this experience and fasted regularly. When it came time for him to appoint elders to the Churches he had established, he sought God through prayer and fasting. Luke said, "Now when they had appointed elders in every church, and prayed with fasting, they commended them to the Lord in whom they had believed" (Acts 14:23). (See also 2 Corinthians 6:5 and 11:27.)

Cornelius was a devout Gentile seeking to know God. He also sought God through prayer and fasting. We read his words in Acts, "So Cornelius said, 'Four days ago I was fasting until this hour; and at the ninth hour I prayed in my house, and behold, a man stood before me in bright clothing, and said, "Cornelius, your prayer has been heard, and your alms are remembered in the sight of God" ' " (Acts 10:30-31).

Fasting as a Way of Life

For the Christian, fasting is not a legalistic endeavor; it is expected as a way of life. Jesus said, "Moreover, when you fast, do not be like the hypocrites, with a sad countenance. For they disfigure their faces that they may appear to men to be fasting . . . " (Matt. 6:16)

Notice that Jesus did not say, "if" you fast. He said "when" you fast! He took it for granted that believers would fast.

When we study the history of Christianity, we discover that serious-minded believers down through the ages have practiced fasting as a means of humbling themselves before God. This includes every man and woman who has made a significant and lasting impact on the Church of Jesus Christ. Shouldn't we also make this important practice a regular part of our lives?

Degrees of Fasting

The Bible seems to indicate three degrees or levels of fasting. These are the normal fast, the limited fast and the extreme fast.

In the normal fast, the person does not eat, but he does drink the necessary liquids. This was apparently the degree of fasting Jesus practiced during His forty-day fast. Matthew pointed out that Jesus was hungry, not thirsty (Matt. 4:2).

God has made our bodies in such a way that the average person can go about forty days without food. (Sometimes I have a problem with forty minutes.) During this time of fasting, the body gets its nourishment from the surplus fat stored in the body. After forty days, the body begins to consume its living cells, and the person will die if the fast is not broken.

I find it interesting that Satan waited until Jesus had fasted the full forty days before he came to tempt Jesus with the bread. This was clearly a real temptation for Jesus, which He was able to overcome through the power of God's Word.

The second degree of fasting recorded in the Bible is the limited fast. In this level of fasting, the person eats some food,

78

but it is limited to a certain type of food. Daniel is an example of a person who practiced this level of fasting.

When Daniel was in Babylon, he and three of his friends were selected for special training to serve the king. They were told to eat certain rich foods as part of their training. These food items had been offered to the Babylonian gods, which meant that Daniel and his friends could not eat them. Daniel made the following request of the steward, "Please test your servants for ten days, and let them give us vegetables to eat and water to drink" (Dan. 1:12).

Can you imagine someone wanting broccoli rather than prime rib?

But at the end of the ten-day period, Daniel and his three companions were in better physical shape than the others who had eaten the "king's dainties."

At another time, Daniel had a vision that troubled him so greatly that he prayed and fasted. We read the following account, "In those days I, Daniel, was mourning three full weeks. I ate no pleasant food, no meat or wine came into my mouth, nor did I anoint myself at all, till three whole weeks were fulfilled" (Dan. 10:2-3).

A more severe level of fasting recorded in the Bible is the extreme fast. In this level of fast, the person neither eats nor drinks.

Moses was on an extreme fast when he received the commandments from God. We read in Exodus, "So he was there with the LORD forty days and forty nights; he neither ate bread nor drank water. And He wrote on the tablets the words of the covenant, the Ten Commandments" (Ex. 34:28). (See also Deuteronomy 9:9.)

Moses repeated this extreme fast when the Hebrews sinned against God by making the golden calf. Moses said, "And I fell down before the LORD, as at the first, forty days and forty nights; I neither ate bread nor drank water, because of all your sin which you committed in doing wickedly in the sight of the LORD, to provoke Him to anger" (Deut. 9:18).

Ezra was grieved because of the sins of the people and fasted in this way. We read, "Then Ezra rose up from before the house of God, and went into the chamber of Jehohanan the son of Eliashib; and when he came there, he ate no bread and drank no water, for he mourned because of the great guilt of those from the captivity" (Ezra 10:6).

In a reference we've already noted, Esther called for an extreme fast when she went in before the king (Esther 4:16).

Types of Fast

A fast may be private or public. An individual fast is a private matter between the person and God. In the Scriptures in Matthew 6:16, Jesus rebuked the religious leaders because they fasted in such a way as to impress the common people. Jesus called them hypocrites.

In ancient times, a hypocrite was an actor who wore a mask to give the appearance that he was someone other than himself. When Jesus called the Pharisees hypocrites, he was accusing them of pretending to be pious when in reality they were only seeking the praise of men.

Individual fasting must be done unto God, not men. (See Zechariah 7:5.) Jesus went on to say, "But you, when you fast, anoint your head and wash your face, so that you do not appear to men to be fasting, but to your Father who is in the secret place; and your Father who sees in secret will reward you openly" (Matt. 6:17-18).

There are times as well when fasting is done collectively and publicly. The Day of Atonement mentioned earlier is an example.

There are also other examples of public fasting mentioned in the Bible. On one occasion, a civil war took place between the armies of the tribe of Benjamin and the other tribes of Israel. The armies of Benjamin won the first two battles. This prompted the entire Israeli army to weep and fast before the Lord. The book of Judges tells us, "Then all the children of Israel, that is, all the people, went up and came to the house of God and wept. They sat there before the LORD and fasted that day until evening . . . " (Judg. 20:26)

Jeremiah instructed his associates to read God's Word on the public fast day (Jer. 36:6). In Scriptures mentioned previously, Joel called the nation to fast because of their sins (Joel 1:14; 2:15). The fast during the time of Esther was also a public fast (Esther 4:13,16). The entire city of Nineveh fasted as a sign of repentance before God (Jon. 3:5).

The United States had its own civil war crisis that threatened to destroy the nation. President Abraham Lincoln, sensing the critical need for God's help, proclaimed a national day of fasting with these words:

> "We have been the recipients of the choicest bounties of heaven. We have been preserved, these many years, in peace and prosperity. We have grown in numbers, wealth and power, as no other nation has ever grown. But we have forgotten God. We have forgotten the gracious hand which preserved us in peace, and multiplied and enriched and strengthened us; and we have vainly imagined, in the deceitfulness of our hearts, that all these blessings were produced by some superior wisdom and virtue of our own. Intoxicated with unbroken success, we have become too self-sufficient to feel the necessity of redeeming and preserving grace, too proud to pray to the

God who made us! It behooves us, then to humble ourselves before the offended power, to confess our national
sins, and to pray for clemency and forgiveness" (from
The Rebirth of America. The Arthur S. Demoss Foundation, page 151).

Getting Started

President Lincoln's words certainly apply to our nation
today. Yet, as bleak as things appear to be, it's not too late for
America to return to God.

But we must do our part! Desperate times call for desperate
measures. If fasting has not been part of your life, please make
it a regular practice along with fervent praying for revival to
come to America through the Church in America.

As a start, it would be helpful to establish a specific time of
fasting on a regular basis, such as a certain meal on a particular
day or a specific day of the week.

Begin your fast on a small scale and then extend it for
longer periods as your body becomes accustomed to going
without food.

If you have a physical problem or take medicine, such as
insulin, you should consult with your physician before attempt-
ing to fast.

There should be a specific burden for which you are fasting,
although a regular fast can be for matters of a general nature
that concern you. God may lead you to establish a public fast
time within your local Church or community as Joel indicated.

As you fast in faith, God will surely hear the cry of your
heart to loose the bonds of wickedness, to undo the heavy
burdens, to let the oppressed go free, and to break every yoke
in your life and the lives of those around you.

Remember, it only takes one person to make a difference!

Chapter 6 — Fasting in Faith
Study Guide 6

1. What is the biblical meaning of fasting?

2. What is the purpose of fasting?

3. State the three degrees of fasting.

4. List the two types of fast.

5. Determine to include fasting as a regular part of your Christian life. Consider the possibility of organizing a public fast within your local Church and community.

7

Preparing the Way

In a previous chapter, I mentioned that Isaiah spoke of a future prophet who would prepare people for the coming of the Lord. The Bible identifies this prophet as John the Baptist.

Matthew wrote of John, "In those days John the Baptist came preaching in the wilderness of Judea saying, 'Repent, for the kingdom of heaven is at hand!' For this is he who was spoken of by the prophet Isaiah, saying: 'The voice of one crying in the wilderness: "Prepare the way of the LORD; Make His paths straight" ' " (Matt. 3:1-3). (See also Mark 1:1-3 and Luke 3:1-6.)

If we just casually read about John the Baptist in the Bible, we could easily get the impression that he was a "weirdo-fanatic" who liked to live by himself except on occasion when he would go in to town to scream at people.

John was certainly not part of high Jewish society, and you would not have found him modeling the latest Jerusalem fashions. He seemed to prefer the company of God over people. He apparently lived alone in the desert, where he developed a fondness for camel hair clothes, leather belts, locusts and wild honey.

But through a careful study of John's life, we discover certain qualities or characteristics that give us valuable insights in to the kind of person God uses to prepare people for the coming of the Lord.

In this chapter, we're going to examine these aspects of John's life and see how they apply to our lives today as we prepare for the coming revival, and the revelation and manifestation of the glory of God.

Called by God

Our first observation is that John was called by God. In addition to Isaiah's prophecy about John, Malachi also spoke of his coming. Malachi wrote these words about the year 425 B.C., "Behold, I send My messenger, and he will prepare the way before Me . . . " (Mal. 3:1)

Malachi further spoke about this forerunner and identified him with Elijah the prophet (Mal. 4:5). For this reason, the Jewish people have expected Elijah, who never died, to return and announce the coming of the Lord. However, the New Testament Scriptures tell us that John the Baptist was the one Malachi spoke about.

The disciples of Jesus asked Him about Malachi's prophecy concerning Elijah. They were wondering why Elijah had not come to announce Jesus to the people. Jesus responded to their question by identifying John the Baptist as the one Malachi was speaking about.

Matthew wrote, "Then Jesus answered and said to them, 'Elijah is truly coming first and will restore all things. But I say to you that Elijah has come already, and they did not know him but did to him whatever they wished. Likewise the Son of Man is also about to suffer at their hands.' Then the disciples understood that He spoke to them of John the Baptist" (Matt. 17:11-13).

Jesus also said of John's message, "And if you are willing to receive it, he is Elijah who is to come" (Matt. 11:14). (See also Luke 1:17 and 7:27.)

John the Baptist was not a self-proclaimed preacher. He didn't wake up one morning with nothing to do and decided to become a preacher. No, he was called by God. God called and sent John for the special purpose of preparing people for the coming of the Lord so that His glory would be revealed to them.

Christians have also been called by God. Like John, we didn't just decide one day to follow Jesus. The same God that called John has also called us. Peter wrote of our calling with these words, "But you are a chosen generation, a royal priesthood, a holy nation, His own special people, that you may proclaim the praises of Him who called you out of darkness into His marvellous light" (1 Pet. 2:9).

We have also been called for a purpose. Paul wrote that God " . . . has saved us and called us with a holy calling, not according to our works, but according to His own purpose and grace which was given to us in Christ Jesus before time began" (2 Tim. 1:9).

We learn further from the book of Romans, "And we know that all things work together for good to those who love God, to those who are the called according to His purpose" (Rom. 8:28).

Yes, God has called us for a purpose. Peter said the purpose for which God has called us is to proclaim His praises on the earth. As we fulfill this purpose both in word and deed, God's glory will be revealed on the earth. Revival will come and lives will be changed.

Born Supernaturally

A second observation about John is that he was born

supernaturally. As with any Jewish couple in the first century, Zacharias and Elizabeth desperately wanted children. But they were not able to have any and had grown beyond the age of childbearing. Luke explains, "But they had no child, because Elizabeth was barren, and they were both well advanced in years" (Luke 1:7).

However, God had something special in mind for Zacharias and Elizabeth. And when it was time, He sent the angel Gabriel to announce to Zacharias that he would soon have a son. Gabriel said that this son was to be the one Isaiah and Malachi had spoken about (Luke 1:16-17). The details of the events leading up to and including John's birth are recorded in the first chapter of the book of Luke.

Christians have also been born supernaturally. Our supernatural birth is of a spiritual nature. One day a religious leader named Nicodemus came to Jesus to learn more about His teachings. Jesus said to him " . . . Most assuredly, I say to you, unless one is born again, he cannot see the kingdom of God" (John 3:3).

Nicodemus was puzzled about what this meant. He could only relate to the natural world. Jesus repeated Himself and explained to Nicodemus that He was talking about a spiritual birth. (See John 3:4-8.)

God has always had something special in mind for those He has called. When it was just the right time, He sent the Holy Spirit to come and live in us, making our spirits come alive to God. We receive the very life of God Himself and are spiritually born again into the family of God.

Filled with the Spirit

One of the most blessed aspects of John's life was that he was filled with God's Spirit while still in his mother's womb.

88

Gabriel said of John, "For he will be great in the sight of the Lord, and he shall drink neither wine nor strong drink. He will also be filled with the Holy Spirit, even from his mother's womb" (Luke 1:15).

John was filled with the Holy Spirit in order to have the anointing of God on his life. This was necessary for John, because it gave him the power he needed to serve God successfully and to fulfill his calling.

John's dependence on the Holy Spirit was more than a one-time experience in his mother's womb. For John, it was a living, dynamic relationship throughout his life. Luke substantiates this for us about John, "So the child grew and became strong in spirit . . . " (Luke 1:80)

We too must be filled with the Holy Spirit in order to fulfill God's calling for our lives and to prepare ourselves and others to see His glory. Luke said it this way, "But you shall receive power when the Holy Spirit has come upon you; and you shall be witnesses to Me in Jerusalem, and in all Judea and Samaria, and to the end of the earth" (Acts 1:8).

This filling or anointing with the Holy Spirit must be more than a one-time experience for us, just as it was for John. Paul expressed it with these words, "And be not drunk with wine, wherein is excess; but be filled with the Spirit" (Eph. 5:18, KJV).

The word which Paul used in the Greek language for our English word "filled" means to be continuously filled with and controlled by God's Spirit as a way of life. Only then are we able to serve God successfully, fulfilling His calling for our lives and striving to be ready for His visitation in the coming revival.

Living a Godly Life

Because John was filled with the Holy Spirit, he was able to live a godly life that both pleased the Lord and convicted those around him who claimed to know God but who didn't live as He demands. We can identify six characteristics of John's life that set him apart and made him useful for God's purpose of bringing revival into the hearts of the people.

1. He Was Able to Hear from God

I mentioned in the earlier chapter on repentance that there was a famine of God's Word in Israel for 400 years. God did not speak to His people because of their disobedience. Even the religious leaders did not hear from God. They simply quoted each other and told the people whatever they wanted to hear.

John was different. He heard from God. Luke recorded this insight about John and said, "while Annas and Caiaphas were high priests, the word of God came to John the son of Zacharias in the wilderness" (Luke 3:2).

I find it interesting that God did not speak to the High Priest (the religious leaders). Instead, he spoke to a man who had no religious education, but who lived a holy life in obedience to God.

It's very important to understand what Luke meant when he said, "the Word of God came to John." Let me explain it to you.

The New Testament was written in the Greek language. The Greek language was much more expressive than the English language is today. Its words had very precise meanings. In the New Testament, there are two different Greek words that when translated into the English Bible are referred to by the phrase, "The Word of God."

The first of these Greek words is "logos." This refers to the general revelation of God in its entirety. Thus the whole Bible may be referred to as the Word of God. It is the general, written revelation from God for everybody.

The second of these Greek words is "rhema." This word refers to a specific personal revelation from God to an individual. It is the Word of God spoken by the Holy Spirit to you personally. In this situation, the Holy Spirit takes the general logos of God (the Bible), which was written for everybody, and makes specific Scriptures come alive to you personally with the very life, authority and power of God Himself. When this happens, you know that God has spoken to you personally. You have received a "Thus saith the Lord" in your spirit.

When Luke wrote that the Word of God came to John, he used the word "rhema." John heard the fresh, living, dynamic Word of God in his spirit because he lived a holy life. He was therefore able to speak God's Word with the authority and power of God so that it changed people's lives when they heard it.

The same God who spoke to John desires to reveal Himself to us. He wants to bring revival to our hearts so that we can see His glory. But we too must live a holy life. We too must be willing to obey God's Word, or else He will not reveal Himself to us.

Jesus said, "He who has My commandments and keeps them, it is he who loves Me. And he who loves Me will be loved by My Father, and I will love him and manifest Myself to him" (John 14:21).

God will speak His Word to us when we are committed to obey it. James wrote, "Therefore lay aside all filthiness and overflow of wickedness, and receive with meekness the implanted word, which is able to save your souls. But be doers of the word, and not hearers only . . . " (James 1:21-22)

When God speaks His rhema Word to us, it carries within it the very life of God Himself. God's Word is so powerful it is able to quicken our dead spirits and make them alive to God. His Word can renew our minds, convict and stabilize our emotions, and empower our wills. God's Word can even bring healing to our bodies.

The writer of Hebrews understood the awesome power of God's Word and wrote, "For the word of God is living and powerful, and sharper than any two-edged sword, piercing even to the division of soul and spirit, and of joints and marrow, and is a discerner of the thoughts and intents of the heart" (Heb. 4:12).

Jesus said: " . . . 'Man shall not live by bread alone, but by every word that proceeds from the mouth of God' " (Matt. 4:4). The Greek word used to record Jesus' statement is rhema. Jesus was talking about the personal word from God that is quickened to our hearts by the Holy Spirit. He even went on to describe this word as coming from the mouth of God.

Beloved, do you want to hear from God? Do you want Him to speak His words of life to you? Then give heed to the following counsel from the Bible, "Trust in the LORD with all your heart, and lean not on your own understanding; in all your ways acknowledge Him, and He shall direct your paths" (Prov. 3:5-6).

2. He Was a Man of Prayer

Another reason God was able to use John is because he was a man of prayer. One day while Jesus was praying, one of His disciples came to Him with the following request: " . . . 'Lord, teach us to pray, as John also taught his disciples' " (Luke 11:1).

You see, when God spoke His rhema word to John, it

burned in John's heart with an all-consuming fire. Once he heard God's Word, John became single-minded. He thought about it constantly, and nothing could distract his attention from obeying what God had told him to do.

But John also knew that the task God had given him was beyond his natural abilities to accomplish. It would not be easy for him to break the 400 years of silence by telling people to repent. It would take great courage to stand alone and rebuke the religious leaders, calling them a bunch of snakes. (See Matthew 3:7 and Luke 3:7.)

I'm sure John learned the importance of prayer in the early days of his life. He must have spent many long hours in prayer, and it was probably during a time of prayer that God spoke to him. John knew the value of prayer and taught his followers to pray.

Jesus' disciple observed that He also spent much time in prayer. He was impressed with the priority John and Jesus gave to prayer and made the request that should concern us all, "Lord, teach us to pray."

The same God that John prayed to is still able to answer our prayers today. As stated earlier, prayer is a prerequisite to revival, and the revelation and manifestation of the glory of God. Perhaps this is why Paul wrote that we should constantly be praying (Eph. 6:18).

Jesus answered His disciple by giving him a model prayer as a guide in praying. We call it "The Lord's prayer," but it is really the disciples' prayer. Jesus specified five elements that should be included in our prayers.

The first element is worship. Worship is simply giving glory to God for who He is in His being. We read in 1 Chronicles 16:29, "Give to the LORD the glory due His name; bring an offering, and come before Him. Oh, worship the LORD in the beauty of holiness!"

The second element Jesus mentioned is praise. Praise is giving glory to God for what He does. The Psalmist wrote, "I will praise You, O LORD my God, with all my heart, and I will glorify Your name forevermore" (Ps. 86:12).

Next, Jesus spoke of the need for confession. We can define confession as simply agreeing with God concerning our needs. John wrote, "If we confess our sins, He is faithful and just to forgive us our sins and to cleanse us from all unrighteousness" (1 John 1:9).

The fourth element Jesus mentioned is intercession. As I said previously, intercession is expressing concern for the needs of others. It is a daily concern for the glory of God and the burdens carried by those around you.

Finally, Jesus included petitions as a necessary part of our prayers. A petition is a specific request to God concerning your own needs. Paul encourages us to give our burdens to God with these words, "Be anxious for nothing, but in everything by prayer and supplication, with thanksgiving, let your requests be made known to God" (Phil. 4:6).

S.D. Gordon once said, "The greatest thing anyone can do for God and man is pray. It is not the only thing, but it is the chief thing. The greatest people of earth are the people who pray. I do not mean those who talk about prayer; nor those who say they believe in prayer; nor yet those who can explain about prayer; but I mean those people who take time to pray" (from *The Rebirth of America*. The Arthur S. Demoss Foundation, page 191).

3. He Practiced Fasting

John was so concerned for the glory of God that he and his

followers often fasted as a way of keeping their attention on spiritual matters. However, Jesus' disciples did not fast. This puzzled one of John's followers who went to Jesus with the following question, " . . . Why do we and the Pharisees fast often, but Your disciples do not fast?" (Matt. 9:14)

Jesus answered, " . . . Can the friends of the bridegroom mourn as long as the bridegroom is with them? But the days will come when the bridegroom will be taken away from them, and then they will fast" (Matt. 9:15).

What Jesus meant by His answer was that His disciples would not fast while He was with them, but they would fast after He returned to heaven.

We learned in an earlier chapter that God honors fasting in our lives when we do it with proper motives. Godly men and women throughout history have practiced fasting as a way of life. The Bible records many instances when God's people became serious about spiritual matters and fasted as an outward means of expressing their inward concerns for God's glory. The result was always a revival in the hearts of the people and a restoration of the glory of God.

Proper fasting can be a channel through which the blessings of God may flow to us. For this reason, Jesus gave the following teaching about fasting in a Scripture we discussed earlier, "Moreover, when you fast, do not be like the hypocrites, with a sad countenance. For they disfigure their faces that they may appear to men to be fasting. Assuredly, I say to you, they have their reward. But you, when you fast, anoint your head and wash your face, so that you do not appear to men to be fasting, but to your Father who is in the secret place; and your Father who sees in secret will reward you openly" (Matt. 6:16-18).

Perhaps you've never practiced fasting on a consistent

basis. My wife and I have for years, and I would like to encourage you to do so as well. You'll discover, as we have, that fasting can be an important prerequisite to a spiritual awakening in your life.

4. He Lived by Faith

A further quality in John's life that made him useful to God was his faith. God called John to prepare people for the coming Messiah. Yet, John himself did not even know the identity of the Messiah. Can you imagine trying to get people to believe in someone when you don't even know who the someone is yourself? John did!

We read the following, "The next day John saw Jesus coming toward him, and said, 'Behold! The Lamb of God who takes away the sin of the world! This is He of whom I said, "After me comes a Man who is preferred before me, for He was before me." I did not know Him; but that He should be revealed to Israel, therefore I came baptizing with water.' And John bore witness, saying, 'I saw the Spirit descending from heaven like a dove, and He remained upon Him. I did not know Him, but He who sent me to baptize with water said to me, "Upon whom you see the Spirit descending, and remaining on Him, this is He who baptizes with the Holy Spirit." And I have seen and testified that this is the Son of God' " (John 1:29-34).

When the Word of God came to John, he prayed and fasted as a means of seeking God's help. It was during these times alone with God that supernatural faith filled his heart. He was then able to boldly proclaim the coming of one greater than he — one that he did not know himself until the time came for God to reveal His identity to John.

We have it so much easier than John because we know the

One about whom we're speaking. We know who the Messiah is because John has identified Him for us as Jesus of Nazareth — the Son of God. Yet, we too must live by faith.

We learn from the writer of Hebrews, "But without faith it is impossible to please Him, for he who comes to God must believe that He is, and that He is a rewarder of those who diligently seek Him" (Heb. 11:6).

This life of faith will be manifested in our lives by works of lovingkindness. James said it this way, "What does it profit, my brethren, if someone says he has faith but does not have works? Can faith save him? If a brother or sister is naked and destitute of daily food, and one of you says to them, 'Depart in peace, be warmed and filled,' but you do not give them the things which are needed for the body, what does it profit? Thus also faith by itself, if it does not have works, is dead. But someone will say, 'You have faith, and I have works.' Show me your faith without your works, and I will show you my faith by my works. For as the body without the spirit is dead, so faith without works is dead also" (James 2:14-18,26).

As we seek God through prayer and fasting, His faith will fill our hearts so that we are able to believe that God can help us accomplish things that are beyond our own natural abilities.

Paul expressed it this way, "For we walk by faith, not by sight" (2 Cor. 5:7).

This God kind of faith produces a spirit of revival in our hearts enabling us to walk with Him at a high level of godliness and holiness, which will have a profound impact on the lives of those around us.

5. He Hated Sin and Hypocrisy

When we think of John the Baptist, it's easy for us to visualize him as a hell-fire and brimstone preacher. I don't know if that is true or not, but one thing is certain, John hated sin and hypocrisy.

Because of God's anointing on John, huge crowds came to hear him preach. Many in the crowds sincerely desired to hear from God. They were hungry for His Word and believed in John's message. They repented of their sins and were baptized as a way of publicly expressing their desire to walk with God.

But not everyone who attended John's meetings was a sincere seeker of God. This was especially true of the religious leaders. They were hypocrites. John knew what was in their hearts, and he was not afraid to publicly rebuke them.

We read the following account in Matthew, "Then Jerusalem, all Judea, and all the region around the Jordan went out to him and were baptized by him in the Jordan, confessing their sins. But when he saw many of the Pharisees and Sadducees coming to his baptism, he said to them, 'Brood of vipers! Who has warned you to flee from the wrath to come? Therefore bear fruits worthy of repentance, and do not think to say to yourselves, "We have Abraham as our father." For I say to you that God is able to raise up children to Abraham from these stones. And even now the ax is laid to the root of the trees. Therefore every tree which does not bear good fruit is cut down and thrown into the fire' " (Matt. 3:5-10).

In order for us to have revival in our lives and see God's glory, we too must hate sin and hypocrisy both in our own lives as well as in the lives of others. We must acknowledge our sins and turn from them, seeking God with sincere hearts.

King David committed a terrible sin against Uriah and Bathsheba. But he acknowledged his sin. He said, "I acknowledged my sin to You, and my iniquity I have not hidden. I said,

'I will confess my transgressions to the LORD,' and You forgave the iniquity of my sin" (Ps. 32:5).

We read in Psalm 66:18, "If I regard iniquity in my heart, the LORD will not hear."

Isaiah wrote, "Behold, the LORD's hand is not shortened, that He cannot save; nor His ear heavy, that it cannot hear. But your iniquities have separated you from your God; and your sins have hidden His face from you, so that He will not hear" (Isa. 59:1-2).

The apostle John expressed it this way, "If we say that we have no sin, we deceive ourselves, and the truth is not in us. If we confess our sins, He is faithful and just to forgive us our sins and cleanse us from all unrighteousness" (1 John 1:8-9).

There are many in the "Church crowd" today who are not sincere seekers of God. They profess to know and love Him, but their lives prove otherwise. They are hypocrites!

You see, beloved, it's not enough to attend Church services on Sunday and sing a few hymns and spiritual songs. We must have such a zeal for God's name and God's honor that we will love righteousness and hate evil. We must live what we say we believe so that our lives are open and blameless before God and man.

Joshua spoke these words to the Hebrews, "Now therefore, fear the LORD, serve Him in sincerity and in truth . . . " (Josh. 24:14) These pointed words certainly apply to us today.

Paul expressed it this way, "Grace be with all those who love our Lord Jesus Christ in sincerity . . . " (Eph. 6:24)

6. He was Humble

The last quality I want to mention about John is that he was humble. It's hard to think of this bold prophet as being humble, but he certainly was, if we understand that to be humble means not to exalt ourselves.

When John preached about the coming Messiah, He always took a subordinate position. He never tried to get people to follow himself. He was not interested in promoting himself nor his ministry. John recognized the temporary nature of his ministry and prepared his listeners to follow the Messiah, not John.

We read the following from part of John's sermon, "I indeed baptize you with water unto repentance, but He who is coming after me is mightier than I, whose sandals I am not worthy to carry . . . " (Matt. 3:11)

These are certainly the words of a man who knew his place.

In the coming revival, God is going to use those who are humble before Him. He will not share His glory with any person or ministry that seeks to exalt itself. He will bring down those people and ministries that promote themselves and tell others what they want to hear in order to get a following. He will bring forth those people and ministries that have walked before Him with humility and humbleness.

After God deals with those in the pulpit, He will then lovingly chastise those who sit comfortably in their pews, everyone who is filled with pride, self-sufficiency and an exaggerated view of their own self-importance.

James wrote of the times when God would do this work in our lives. He said, "Lament and mourn and weep! Let your laughter be turned to mourning and your joy to gloom. Humble yourselves in the sight of the Lord, and He will lift you up" (James 4:9-10).

Isaiah added these words, "But this is the man to whom I will look, he that is humble and contrite in spirit, and trembles at my word" (Isa. 66:2, RSV).

Pointing People to Jesus

There are numerous observations we could make about John the Baptist. But perhaps the most important one is that he pointed people to Jesus.

The apostle John wrote of John the Baptist, "There was a man sent from God, whose name was John. This man came for a witness, to bear witness of the Light, that all through him might believe. He was not that Light, but was sent to bear witness of that Light. John bore witness of Him and cried out, saying, 'This was He of whom I said, "He who comes after me is preferred before me, for He was before me" ' " (John 1:6-8,15).

When John realized that Jesus was the Messiah, he said of Jesus, " . . . Behold! the Lamb of God who takes away the sin of the world! This is whom I said, 'After me comes a Man who is preferred before me, for He was before me.' . . . And I have seen and testified that this is the Son of God" (John 1:29-30,34).

The following day John again saw Jesus and repeated his statement which resulted in Jesus' first disciples. We read, "Again, the next day, John stood with two of his disciples. And looking at Jesus as He walked, he said, 'Behold the Lamb of God!' The two disciples heard him speak, and they followed Jesus" (John 1:35-37).

When God brings revival, there is always a renewed focus on Jesus Christ. God does not exalt religious denominations, traditions, doctrines, ministries or human personalities. He sends His Spirit to draw people to Jesus Christ.

The witness God gives to Jesus relates to His person, His work and His necessity.

Regarding the person of Jesus, the Bible clearly and boldly

declares Him to be God in human flesh. Paul expressed it with these words, "For in Him [Christ] dwells all the fullness of the Godhead bodily [in bodily form]" (Col. 2:9).

Concerning the work of Jesus, the Bible tells us that He came to save us from our sins and reconcile us to God. Paul wrote: " . . . God was in Christ reconciling the world to Himself, not imputing their trespasses to them, and has committed to us the word of reconciliation" (2 Cor. 5:19).

In considering the necessity of Jesus, the Lord Himself said, "I am the way, the truth, and the life. No one comes to the Father except through Me" (John 14:6).

Luke added these words about Jesus, "Nor is there salvation in any other, for there is no other name under heaven given among men by which we must be saved" (Acts 4:12).

Paul contributed this statement, "For there is one God and one Mediator between God and men, the Man Christ Jesus" (1 Tim. 2:5).

I hope there are some good things people could say about my life. But of all the things they might say, the most important to me is, "He pointed people to Jesus."

Dying to Self

In order for John to prepare people to follow Jesus, he had to first die to himself. By this I mean John had to lay aside his own desires and ambitions so that God's plan might be accomplished through him.

For a brief period, John and Jesus ministered at the same time. This naturally caused some confusion among the people, but particularly with John's followers. I'm sure they were concerned that Jesus' growing popularity would bring John's ministry to an end. Of course! That was God's plan. It was supposed to happen that way.

The apostle John recorded the following conversation between John the Baptist and some of his followers. "And they came to John and said to him, 'Rabbi, He who was with you beyond the Jordan, to whom you have testified — behold, He is baptizing, and all are coming to Him!' John answered and said, ' . . . You yourselves bear me witness, that I have said, "I am not the Christ," but, "I have been sent before Him" . . . He must increase, but I must decrease' " (John 3:26-30).

John never desired a following. He wasn't interested in getting disciples for himself. He did not want the crowds to idolize him. He did not care about having a permanent ministry. So he never built a building or established an organization bearing his name. He simply wanted people to follow Jesus. In fact, John's success was determined by how many people left him to follow Jesus.

Jesus was the perfect example of one who died to Himself. He said, "For I came down from heaven, not to do My own will, but the will of Him who sent Me" (John 6:38).

He calls all who would follow Him to do the same. Jesus gave these instructions for our understanding, " . . . If anyone desires to come after Me, let him deny himself, and take up his cross daily, and follow Me. For whoever desires to save his life will lose it, but whoever loses his life for My sake will save it" (Luke 9:23-24).

Jesus spoke of taking up our crosses daily. Many people misunderstand what Jesus meant by those words. They think He was talking about being poor or miserable in order to be holy. But this is not at all what He meant.

To understand the meaning of Jesus' words requires us to understand them as His listeners would have understood them in the first century. If you lived in Jesus' time and saw someone carrying his own cross, you knew that person was going to die. The phrase "take up your cross daily" simply means to die to yourself.

To whom will God reveal Himself? It will be to the one who has the same desires concerning Jesus which John expressed, the one whose deepest yearning is for more of Jesus and less of self.

Giving Your Life

Because John had an eternal view of his life and ministry, he was not afraid to speak the truth regardless of who it offended.

King Herod greatly admired John. But he feared him because John spoke with the authority of God and was popular with the people. (See Matthew 14:5 and Mark 6:20.)

Herod had many weaknesses, one of which was women. He lived in adultery with his brother's wife, Herodias. John rebuked Herod for this and made his life miserable. When Herodias' daughter performed a lewd dance before Herod, he was over-come with lust and promised her anything she wanted. At her mother's prompting, she asked for the head of John the Baptist. Although this grieved Herod, he could not break his promise. He had John beheaded and presented his head to the girl, on a platter, as she requested. (See Matthew 14:1-12.)

John was a man of great convictions. He knew he spoke the Word of God, and he gave his life for what he believed.

Throughout history, whenever there has been a fresh move of God, it has always been ridiculed by the unbelieving world and rejected by the established religious structures. The coming revival will be no exception.

There will be strong opposition to the next move of God.

This will not only come from the secular world, but much of it will also be from the religious community.

The truth is never popular. But we must be prepared to declare it whatever the cost. We must have godly convictions to speak His Word no matter who we offend.

Jesus said, "Blessed are those who are persecuted for righteousness' sake, for theirs is the kingdom of heaven. Blessed are you when they revile and persecute you, and say all kinds of evil against you falsely for My sake. Rejoice and be exceedingly glad, for great is your reward in heaven, for so they persecuted the prophets who were before you" (Matt. 5:10-12).

Paul wrote, "Yes, and all who desire to live godly in Christ Jesus will suffer persecution" (2 Tim. 3:12).

But Paul also gave us these words of encouragement: "If we endure, we shall also reign with Him" (2 Tim. 2:12); "For I consider that the sufferings of this present time are not worthy to be compared with the glory which shall be revealed in us" (Rom. 8:18).

The Greatest Honor of All

The last observation I want to make about John's life concerns the incredible honor Jesus gave to him. Luke recorded these words from Jesus about John, "For I say to you, among those born of women there is not a greater prophet than John the Baptist; but he who is least in the kingdom of God is greater than he" (Luke 7:28).

Apparently, Jesus honored John the Baptist so highly because John was his immediate forerunner, who lived a godly life and paid the supreme price of his own life so that Jesus would be exalted.

There were many great prophets who preceded John. They all spoke in faith about the coming Messiah. But their understanding of the full meaning of their own prophecies was limited (1 Pet. 1:10-12). John was the prophet who had the privilege of actually knowing the One about whom all the other prophets spoke. And because he was faithful to his calling, Jesus honored him above all his predecessors.

Yet, with the same breath, Jesus said that the least in the kingdom of God would be greater than John. That's certainly an incredible statement! What did He mean, and how does His statement relate to our lives?

Jesus, Himself, gave us the answer, and both Matthew and Luke recorded it for us. Matthew wrote, "Therefore whoever confesses Me before men, him I will also confess before My Father who is in heaven" (Matt. 10:32). Luke added the following detail, "Also I say to you, whoever confesses Me before men, him the Son of Man will confess before the angels of God" (Luke 12:8).

Jesus confessed John before the people. He will confess us before God and the angels in heaven. And we will rule and reign with Him throughout eternity.

What will Jesus confess to God and the angels about you? Here are His own words: " . . . Well done, good and faithful servant; you were faithful over a few things, I will make you ruler over many things. Enter into the joy of your Lord" (Matt. 25:21,23).

Chapter 7 — Preparing the Way
Study Guide 7

1. What qualities and characteristics should we have in our lives in order for God to use us to prepare the way for Him?

2. Why should Jesus say to you, "Well done, good and faithful servant"?

3. What must you do to prepare yourself for a divine visitation in the coming revival?

BIBLE STUDY MATERIALS BY RICHARD BOOKER

MINISTRY IN THE LOCAL CHURCH
Richard currently spends most of his time in a traveling ministry to the local church. If you are interested in having him come to your church, contact him directly at his Houston address.

CHRISTIAN GROWTH SEMINARS
Richard conducts a series of unique seminars in the local church. Each seminar is six hours long with a workbook in which the participant writes during the seminar. Current seminars are on prayer, personal Bible study, successful Christian living, and discipleship. Brochures are available from the ministry.

LOCAL CHURCH CENTERED BIBLE SCHOOLS
Richard has developed a Christian Growth Institute, which is a nine-month Bible school designed to be taught in the local church by the pastor or his associates. A catalog is available from the ministry.

BOOKS
Richard's books are superior quality teaching books. They uniquely communicate profound life-changing Bible truths with a rich depth, freshness and simplicity, and also explain how to apply what you have read to your life. His books are described on the following pages. You may order them through your bookstore or clip and mail the Book Order Form provided in the back of this book.

THE MIRACLE OF THE SCARLET THREAD
This book explains how the Old and New Testaments are woven together by the scarlet thread of the blood covenant to tell one complete story through the Bible.

COME AND DINE
This book takes the mystery and confusion out of the Bible. It provides background information on how we got the Bible, a survey of every book in the Bible and how each relates to Jesus Christ, practical principles, forms and guidelines for your own personal Bible study, and a systematic plan for effectively reading, studying and understanding the Bible for yourself.

INTIMACY WITH GOD
This book is about the God of the Bible. It shows the ways in which God has revealed Himself to us and explains the attributes, plans and purposes of God. Then each attribute is related practically to the reader. This book takes you into the very heart of God and demonstrates how to draw near to Him.

RADICAL CHRISTIAN LIVING
This book explains how you can grow to become a mature Christian and help others do so as well. You'll learn the pathway to Christian maturity and how to select and train others in personal follow-up and discipling at different levels of Christian growth.

SEATED IN HEAVENLY PLACES
This book helps the reader learn how to live the victorious Christian life and walk in the power of God. It explains how to minister to others, wear the armor of God and exercise spiritual authority.

BLOW THE TRUMPET IN ZION
This book explains the dramatic story of God's covenant plan for Israel, including their past glory and suffering, their present crisis and their future hope.

JESUS IN THE FEASTS OF ISRAEL
This book is a study of the Old Testament feasts showing how they pointed to Jesus, as well as their personal and prophetic significance for today's world. The book points out how the Feasts represent seven steps to Christian growth and the peace, power and rest of God.

HOW TO PREPARE FOR THE COMING REVIVAL

There is a great expectancy in the hearts of believers everywhere that we are on the threshold of a great revival that will soon shake the world. This book explains the true meaning of revival and what we must do to prepare ourselves for a visitation from God.

AUDIO CASSETTE TAPE ALBUMS

A list of Richard's teaching cassettes is included on the following pages. All tape series come in an attractive album for your convenience. To order tapes, check the appropriate box, then clip and mail the Order Form which is provided on the last page of this book following the tape list.

BOOK ORDER FORM

Ordering Instructions

To order books, check the appropriate box, then clip and mail the coupon below to SOUNDS OF THE TRUMPET, INC., 8230 BIRCHGLENN, HOUSTON, TX 77070.

☐ Please send me _____ copy(ies) of THE MIRACLE OF THE SCARLET THREAD. I have enclosed $6.95 contribution for each copy ordered (price includes shipping).

☐ Please send me _____ copy(ies) of COME AND DINE. I have enclosed $6.95 contribution for each copy ordered (price includes shipping).

☐ Please send me _____ copy(ies) of INTIMACY WITH GOD. I have enclosed $6.95 contribution for each copy ordered (price includes shipping).

☐ Please send me _____ copy(ies) of RADICAL CHRISTIAN LIVING. I have enclosed $6.95 contribution for each copy ordered (price includes shipping).

☐ Please send me _____ copy(ies) of SEATED IN HEAVENLY PLACES. I have enclosed $6.95 contribution for each copy ordered (price includes shipping).

☐ Please send me _____ copy(ies) of BLOW THE TRUMPET IN ZION. I have enclosed $6.95 contribution for each copy ordered (price includes shipping).

☐ Please send me _____ copy(ies) of JESUS IN THE FEASTS OF ISRAEL. I have enclosed $6.95 contribution for each copy ordered (price includes shipping).

☐ Please send me _____ copy(ies) of HOW TO PREPARE FOR THE COMING REVIVAL. I have enclosed $6.95 contribution for each copy ordered (price includes shipping).

☐ Foreign order please include an extra $2.00 per book for surface postage.

_____

Name _____

Street _____

City _____

State _____ Zip _____

BOOK ORDER FORM

TAPE LIST

■ *The Bible Series*
BL1   Uniqueness of the Bible
BL2   How the Books Became the Book
BL3   Survey of Old Testament
BL4   Survey of New Testament
BL5   How We Got Our English Bible
BL6   Getting Into the Bible
BL7   How to Study the Bible
BL8   How to Understand the Bible

■ *Getting to Know God —1*
KG1   Knowing God
KG2   The Self-Existing One
KG3   The Personal Spirit
KG4   The Trinity

■ *Getting to Know God — 2*
KG1   God Is Sovereign
KG2   God Is All Power
KG3   God Is All Knowledge
KG4   God Is Everywhere Present
KG5   God Never Changes

■ *Getting to Know God — 3*
KG1   God Is Holy
KG2   God Is Love
KG3   God Is Just
KG4   God Is Good

■ *Blood Covenant Series*
BC1   The Blood Covenant
BC2   What Was It Abraham Believed?
BC3   The Tabernacle
BC4   The Sacrifices
BC5   The High Priest
BC6   The Passover

■ *Abundant Life Series*
AL1   Knowing Your Dominion
AL2   Identify with Christ
AL3   Appropriating His Lordship
AL4   Walking in the Spirit
AL5   Ministering in the Spirit
AL6   Wearing the Armor

■ *The Church Series*
CH1   The Church
CH2   The Body of Christ
CH3   Gifts of the Spirit
CH4   Equipping the Saints
CH5   Work of the Ministry
CH6   Building Up the Body

■ *Christian Family Series*
CF1   God's Purpose for Family
CF2   The Husband's Role
CF3   The Wife's Role
CF4   Parent & Children Roles

■ *Faith & Healing Series*
FH1   Divine Healing Today
FH2   Basis for Claiming Healing
FH3   Barriers to Healing

■ *End Time Series*
ET1   Coming World Events — 1
ET2   Coming World Events — 2
ET3   Judgment of Christians
ET4   Seven-Year Tribulation
ET5   Second Coming of Christ
ET6   Millennium
ET7   Great White Throne Judgment
ET8   New Heaven & New Earth

■ *The Feasts Series Tabernacles*
FE1   Passover
FE2   Unleavened Bread
FE3   Pentecost
FE4   Trumpets
FE5   Atonement
FE6   Tabernacles

■ *Sacrifices Series*
SF1   Sin Offering
SF2   Trespass Offering
SF3   Burnt Offering
SF4   Meal Offering
SF5   Peace Offering

■ *Get Your Prayers Answered*
PR1 Introduction to Prayer
PR2 Principles of Prayer
PR3 Why Prayers Aren't Answered
PR4 Persistence in Prayer
PR5 Intercessory Prayer
PR6 Fasting and Prayer

■ *Ephesians Series*
EP1 Background & Blessing
EP2 Prayer for Enlightenment
EP3 New Life in Christ
EP4 Who Is the Seed of Abraham?
EP5 Prayer for Enablement
EP6 Christian Unity
EP7 Ministering to the Saints
EP8 Ministry of the Saints
EP9 Shedding the Graveclothes
EP10 Imitating the Father
EP11 God's Order for Family
EP12 Spiritual Warfare

■ *Philippians Series*
PH1 Background & Prayer
PH2 Victory in Tribulation
PH3 Keys to Unity
PH4 Honoring One Another
PH5 True Righteousness
PH6 Going On with God
PH7 Standing Together
PH8 Sufficiency of God

■ *Colossians Series*
CO1 Background
CO2 Person & Work of Christ
CO3 Christ in You
CO4 Sufficiency of Christ
CO5 Christ Our Life
CO6 New Man in Christ
CO7 Christ in the Home
CO8 Christ outside the Home

■ *Thessalonians Series*
TH1 Background & Prayer
TH2 A Winning Defense
TH3 A Welcome Report
TH4 Walking to Please God
TH5 The Day of the Lord
TH6 Background & Prayer
TH7 Day of the Lord Again
TH8 No Bums Allowed

■ *Practical Studies — 1*
PS1 Living by Faith
PS2 Guidance
PS3 Prayer
PS4 Fasting
PS5 Meditation
PS6 Stewardship

■ *Single Messages (Circle Below)*
SM1 Why God Had To Become Man
SM2 Who Was That God Begat?
SM3 Feasts of the Lord
SM4 Philemon
SM5 Lord's Prayer
SM6 Handling Worry
SM7 Knowing God's Will
SM8 Spiritual Leprosy
SM9 Praying in the Name
SM10 Bible Baptisms
SM11 Signs of His Coming
SM12 Times of The Gentiles
SM13 Christian Giving
SM14 Master Theme of Bible
SM15 The Dominant Force
SM16 Personal Testimony
SM17 Call to Discipleship
SM18 Where Are the Dead?

■ *Foundational Studies — 1*
FS1 Knowing the Bible
FS2 Knowing God
FS3 Knowing Jesus Christ
FS4 Knowing the Holy Spirit
FS5 Knowing Man
FS6 Knowing the Enemy

■ *Foundational Studies — 2*
FS1 Living the Abundant Life
FS2 Water Baptism
FS3 Communion
FS4 Nature of the Church
FS5 The End Times
FS6 Life After Death

■ *Practical Studies — 2*
PS1 Handling Trials
PS2 Sharing Your Faith
PS3 Worship
PS4 Praise
PS5 Health and Healing
PS6 Family Life

TAPE ORDER FORM

Ordering Instructions

To order tapes, check the appropriate box, then clip and mail the coupon below to SOUNDS OF THE TRUMPET, INC., 8230 BIRCHGLENN, HOUSTON, TX 77070.

· ·

☐ Please send me the following tapes. I have enclosed a $4.00 contribution for each tape ordered (No C.O.D.), plus $2.00 for mailing for each tape series.

☐ The Bible Series	($32.00)	☐ The Feasts Series	($24.00)
☐ Getting To Know God — 1	($16.00)	☐ The Sacrifices Series	($20.00)
☐ Getting To Know God — 2	($20.00)	☐ Love Notes from Jesus	($28.00)
☐ Getting To Know God — 3	($16.00)	☐ Ephesians Series	($48.00)
☐ Blood Covenant Series	($24.00)	☐ Philippians Series	($32.00)
☐ Abundant Life Series	($24.00)	☐ Colossians Series	($32.00)
☐ The Church Series	($24.00)	☐ Thessalonians Series	($32.00)
☐ The Christian Family	($16.00)	☐ Single Messages (Circle)	
☐ Faith & Healing Series	($12.00)	(SM 1, 2, 3, 4, 5, 6, 7	($4.00 each)
☐ End Times Series	($32.00)	8, 9, 10, 11, 12, 13	
☐ Prayer Series	($24.00)	14, 15, 16, 17, 18)	
☐ Foundational Studies — 1	($24.00)	☐ Practical Studies — 1	($24.00)
☐ Foundational Studies — 2	($24.00)	☐ Practical Studies — 2	($24.00)

Name _____

Street _____

City _____

State _____ ZIP_____